PATTERNS OF SPANISH PRONUNCIATION

OF SPANISH PRONUNCIATION

A Drillbook

By J. DONALD BOWEN *and* ROBERT P. STOCKWELL

 THE UNIVERSITY OF CHICAGO PRESS

CHICAGO & LONDON

Library of Congress Catalog Card Number: 60:16841

The University of Chicago Press, Chicago and London
The University of Toronto Press, Toronto 5, Canada

© *1960 by The University of Chicago. Published 1960*
Third Impression 1963
Composed and printed by The University of Chicago Press
Chicago, Illinois, U.S.A.

ACKNOWLEDGMENTS

We developed the exercises in this book, and the phonological analysis on which they are based, in part while we were members of the linguistic staff of the School of Languages of the Foreign Service Institute, Department of State, during which time we, with the staff that we supervised, prepared the FSI Spanish, Basic Course (U. S. Government Printing Office). Various ones of these drills appear also in that volume. FSI Spanish, however, is not available outside the government. For the opportunity to experiment with the teaching of pronunciation in large-scale intensive language programs, we wish to acknowledge our debt to the School of Languages and to our former colleagues. For their help in preparing and testing many of these drills, we are particularly grateful to the speakers of Spanish who did the day-by-day classroom teaching there.

TABLE OF CONTENTS

4.27   Choice questions   120
4.28   Deliberate—with pitch drop after /ǀ/   122
4.28.1   Deliberate—with no pitch drop after /ǀ/   123
4.29   Errors resulting from specific English influence—sentence
          modifiers   125
4.29.1   Errors resulting from specific English influence—leavetakings   126
4.3   Complex Intonation Patterns   128
4.31   A common three-phrase sentence pattern   128
4.32   Language in context   130
4.4   Summing-up of Intonation   131

PHONETIC SYMBOLS   133
INDEX   135

INTRODUCTION

This book deals with the problems English speakers have in pronouncing Spanish. It is a book of exercises, with relatively few explanations. The explanations are as simple as it is possible to make them without substantial loss of accuracy.

One of the opinions often found in the schools of the United States is that Spanish is an easy language for Americans to pronounce. The opinion evidently results from the fact that the spelling system with which the sounds of Spanish are written is a fairly good one. It is not perfect, but even if it were perfect it would not make the sounds any easier for Americans to imitate. Pronunciation is a problem quite apart from reading or writing. It deserves study in and of itself, just as the writing system deserves study. The two should not be confused.

English speakers have trouble pronouncing Spanish because Spanish sounds are different from those of English. An American who begins to study Spanish after his sixteenth year has experienced a certain degree of hardening of his linguistic arteries. His habits are established well below the level of awareness, well below the level of conscious control. His way of talking is a socially conditioned set of habit patterns. Not only has his experience severely limited the particular kinds of sounds he makes when he talks, but also this experience has imposed almost unbelievable restrictions on what kinds of sounds he can discriminate when he listens. The process of learning to pronounce a language is as much one of learning what sounds to ignore as it is one of learning what sounds to produce.

In developing a satisfactory pronunciation of Spanish, the American must learn (1) to hear and imitate several sounds that are completely new to him, (2) to ignore the differences between several sounds that are completely familiar to him, and (3) to modify his manner of making most of the other sounds that are familiar to him.

The place to start learning to make a Spanish sound is with the English sound that is closest to it. When the American can actually hear and recognize what the English sound closest to a Spanish one is, and can understand how it is different from the one he should be making, then he is ready to reduce this understanding to the level of habit response. By imitation of an adequate model such as a native speaker, a non-native speaker who talks with little accent, or a recording made by such persons, the proper habits can be established. The imitation, in order to be fruitful, must be at full normal speed of utterance, and every fault must be corrected immediately and insistently.

The efficiency with which such imitation produces results can be stepped up enormously if the material for imitation is so arranged as to highlight the point on which

1

the imitation needs to be focused. One especially effective device is to arrange items in pairs which differ at only one point. These are minimal contrasts. Another device is to arrange items in pairs or triads in which all the same sounds occur but in different sequences.

Besides the necessity for arranging the material to highlight the points of difficulty, it is useful to provide a set of written symbols for the student to look at while he listens. These symbols must correlate perfectly with the things that are there to be listened to. The symbols are a <u>respelling</u> device to be used as an <u>aid</u> <u>to</u> <u>listening</u>. They cannot properly be called a phonetic key to pronunciation for two reasons: first, because a thoroughly phonetic spelling would be infinitely more complex and, second, because the respelling should ordinarily not be used for pronunciation at all—only for listening. The symbols are not a phonemic transcription, since certain allophones are systematically represented as they would not be in a phonemic transcription. The respelling is a pedagogical tool. It is arrived at by comparing the sound systems of Spanish and English to see what the problems will be, and then empirically modifying the transcription through classroom experience until the most useful one is found. The respelling used in this text has been six years in the making. It is undoubtedly still imperfect, but it has certain real advantages.

Because the only objective of these drills is pronunciation, the meaning of the utterances is of no importance. Translations will therefore not be found in this book except in one drill (1.11) where it was thought worthwhile to indicate just how badly a person can be misunderstood if he mixes up different levels of stress. To burden a student with translations would distract his attention from the real point. For practical purposes the utterances may just as well be considered nonsense sequences of noises that happen to be identical with those that are made by speakers of Spanish. But though the meanings themselves are not important, the fact that each member of the pair has a different meaning must be remembered at all times.

We believe that for practical teaching purposes <u>some</u> distinctions in Spanish are more important to master than others. The drills are therefore arranged in a carefully ordered hierarchy of importance. Except that intonation comes up again at the end of the drills, the order in which the drills occur is the order of their importance for learning purposes. On any given utterance it is recommended that correction be imposed in the same sequence, and that the student focus his listening selectively also in the same sequence.

The book presents, then, these components for learning the pronunciation of Spanish:

1. Notes about the differences between the comparable sounds of each language.
2. Descriptions of the articulation of Spanish sounds not present in English.
3. The problems arranged in a hierarchy of importance from most important to least important.
4. A respelling of Spanish that symbolizes consistently each problematic detail.
5. Lists of items that illustrate the distribution of the sounds.
6. Extensive examples for classroom drill on all the problems, each drill ar-

ranged to focus attention on the specific problem it is designed to help the student overcome.

These pronunciation drills can be used at the beginning of any elementary course, or scattered along with other materials through a semester or more of such an elementary course, or as a quick review for intermediate students, or to break improper habits that have been formed by advanced students. They can effectively improve the pronunciation of any person whose pronunciation is not already native. They are not designed as the sole teaching materials for any single course. They are supplementary and have a highly restricted, but crucial, objective: to teach a student how to pronounce Spanish as nearly as possible the way Spanish speakers pronounce it.

We do not feel that correct pronunciation is just a convenient social grace. We assume, as many competent language teachers and well-motivated students assume, that fluent and accurate pronunciation is fundamental to linguistic accomplishment. We hope these materials will lead the student to speak Spanish with less foreign accent and greater awareness of the ways in which Spanish sounds are different from English.

SUGGESTIONS FOR USING THIS BOOK

It is the aim of this book to provide practice material designed to overcome pronunciation problems systematically and efficiently. It is, however, only practice material, a teaching aid. It cannot replace an instructor; if used properly, it can make an instructor's work easier and more productive.

The instructor has two important roles to play in directing the practice sessions for which these exercises are intended:

1. To act as a model.—Nothing in learning a language is more important than a good model, a correct example. Models can be either live or recorded. The exercises in this book are ideally adapted for use in language laboratories because they are not merely words and sentences for students to imitate but words and sentences arranged for selective imitation, for guided imitation, so that the student's attention is continuously focused on the crucial problems. Whether the model for imitation is the teacher in the classroom or the loud-speaker or headphones in the audio laboratory, the model is indispensable to make the marks on paper come alive.

2. To provide guidance and correction.—The teaching of language through television and audio laboratories cannot replace the key function of the instructor in the classroom: to call the student's attention to mistakes and to direct his practice back into correct channels. Also such responsibilities as pacing, encouragement, and stimulation of interest can be met only through personal contact, in the give-and-take context of the classroom.

The practice exercises contained here are of three types, requiring slightly differing procedures. The procedures we describe below are conceived for the classroom, but essentially the same format, omitting choral repetition, may be recorded for use in language laboratories, with time allotted on the recordings for students to make their responses. The three types, with procedures, are these:

1. Pattern drills.—In chapters 1 and 4, longer phrases and whole sentences marked for intonation appear. It is intended that student attention in these should be focused entirely on features of stress, pitch, juncture, and rhythm. That is why in the first chapter all really difficult sequences of consonants and vowels have been carefully omitted. We want the student to get some insight into the lilt, the movement, of Spanish phrases before he begins worrying about details. The procedure should therefore be some variation

4

on the following pattern:

a) Model says the sentence, at normal tempo.
b) Class imitates in chorus.
c) Model repeats the sentence, pointing to an individual student.
d) Student repeats the sentence.
e) Model says second sentence.
f) Class imitates.
g) Model repeats the sentence, pointing to second student.
h) Student repeats the sentence.

(Follow the same procedure throughout the exercise.)

After once through an exercise, or even earlier, if the class is not too large, the choral repetition may be omitted, the instructor simply giving a sentence from the exercise and indicating that a specific student repeat. The exercise should be so conducted as to achieve a regular rhythm: model - student - model - student - model - student. Since each exercise contains many sentences of exactly the same type, there is no need to use the same sentence with each student, which would become monotonous. Different sentences of the same type will achieve the rhythmic uniformity that is needed, but without monotony.

2. Comparison drills.—In chapters 2 and 3, English words are listed parallel with Spanish words. These are intended to help the student grasp the specific phonetic nature of a Spanish sound by comparing it closely with the most nearly similar English sound. There is no necessary similarity in meaning between the words of the two lists, only a similarity in sound. There are two quite different procedures for using these lists of comparisons, emerging from two quite different pedagogical philosophies. The first is this:

a) A student is designated as an assistant for the drill. He says the first English word.
b) The teacher says the first Spanish word, and students focus their attention on trying to hear the difference between the two.
c) The class repeats the Spanish word in chorus.
d) The teacher says the Spanish word again, designating an individual student to repeat.
e) Student repeats.

(Follow the same procedure throughout the exercise.)

After once through an exercise, if the class is not too large, choral repetition may be omitted. The above procedure does not require that the students say both the English word and the similar-sounding Spanish word; it requires that the students listen to the English word, compare it with the Spanish, and then repeat the Spanish. We suggest this procedure because we know that many teachers do not believe that students should be asked to jump from one language to the other—that to ask them to do so is to invite an insidious influence into the classroom. We think such may indeed be true, and we have written the instructions at the head of each comparison drill in accord with this belief. However, it is possible that in some situations a different procedure may produce better results. This is the second procedure:

a) A student is designated as an assistant for this drill. He says the first English word.

b) The teacher says the first Spanish word.

c) The class imitates both the English and Spanish words, attempting to <u>feel</u> as well as <u>hear</u> the difference between them.

d) The two items are modeled as above.

e) An individual student repeats both as above.

(Follow the same procedure throughout the exercise.)

At the end of this procedure, it would be well to return and repeat the list of Spanish words chorally and individually. But it must be remembered that the mistakes students make come directly from the influence of English. They must become <u>aware</u> of this influence in order to overcome it—hence the second procedure above.

3. <u>Contrast drills.</u>—In chapters 2 and 3, Spanish words are listed parallel with other Spanish words that differ from the first one <u>in only one sound, or in the sequence in which the sounds appear</u>. The contrast between any given pair is a <u>minimal</u>, or in some instances near-minimal, contrast. A good procedure for practicing these contrasts is this:

a) The teacher says both members of a pair, being careful to say them exactly alike in intonation and stress, the only difference being the minimal consonantal or vocalic distinction.

b) The students repeat in chorus.

c) The teacher repeats the pair, designating an individual student.

d) The student repeats.

(Follow the same procedure throughout the exercise.)

As usual, choral repetition may be cut out at any point where the individual repetitions are sufficiently good not to need choral reinforcement.

There are several <u>general</u> suggestions which apply throughout all stages of practice and correction.

1. Neither teacher nor student should ever pronounce slowly or in an exaggerated manner. A model of normal rate and tempo must be constantly before the student.

2. Practice should be kept lively; the student should not have time to think or to be bored. If a student's repetition is wrong, the teacher should correct it briefly, have the student repeat, and then move on.

3. The example for imitation should be constantly renewed by the model; one student should not be allowed to use another student's repetition as his model.

4. Since these drills are systematically arranged to cover all difficulties at an appropriate time, the teacher's correction of errors in any one drill should be selectively restricted to the point at issue in that drill—except that as the class progresses through the book, and more and more habits are accumulated, correction at later stages should include what was covered earlier.

5. A useful sequence for presentation and correction is this:

a) <u>Imitation.</u>—Many students are good mimics and need no more than a model and a chance to repeat after the model. But if they are not good mimics, then:

b) <u>Guidance where.</u>—The student's mistake should be isolated. <u>Where</u> in the word did it occur, which syllable, which sound? This can be done by repeating the problematic syllable (being careful to maintain the pronunciation of the syllable in its fuller context), then the whole word, and giving the student another chance at it. If this still results in error, then:

c) Guidance how.—Brief phonetic advice can be given to guide the student toward correct imitation: "lower the tongue," "make the sound voiced," "be sure the tongue touches the teeth," "round your lips more," etc. Eight or ten such correction-phrases do not presume much phonetic knowledge on the part of the student, but they can guide him quickly to eliminate phonetic errors. If this guidance is still not sufficient, then:

d) Guidance why.—At this point, when all else fails, and only at this point, should detailed phonetic explanation be given of the details of the structure of English that the student is imposing on the structure of Spanish.

6. Finally, a problem may be practiced either too much or too little. The utmost caution must be observed to stay clear of either extreme.

A note about symbols.—In general we have tried to use symbols in graphically obvious or standard values; whenever a symbol is used in a way that is neither obvious nor standard, we have explained it in the text. There are a few conventions which are not actually explained, because they are matters of technical linguistic accuracy rather than pedagogical utility. One of these is the use of [square brackets] and /diagonal lines/. The brackets enclose symbols that are phonetic in meaning, whereas the diagonals enclose symbols that are phonemic in meaning. This distinction between phonetic facts and phonemic facts is implicit throughout the drills, even though there is little value in making an explicit point of it. Briefly, phonemic symbols represent the minimum phonetic essentials of a language's pronunciation; phonetic symbols represent details of pronunciation that are beyond this minimum essential level, and linguistically predictable in terms of it. The failure to make a phonemic distinction will always result in the production of a significant error; the failure to give the phonemic distinction the correct phonetic shading may also result in a significant error, but not necessarily.

THE ELEMENTS 1
OF INTONATION

Intonation is a technical term used to describe the various kinds of voice inflection that occur along with the vowels and consonants. It has three main components:

1. Some syllables are more prominent than others. There are two degrees of prominence in Spanish.
2. Some syllables are higher in pitch than others. There are three levels of pitch in Spanish.
3. When a phrase or a whole utterance comes to an end, the end may rise, or fall, or stay level.

These three components are called stress, pitch, and juncture. Every time anyone says anything in Spanish, all three are present. It would be desirable to separate them completely in order to learn to hear them and reproduce them accurately. But since all are inevitably present in every utterance, the best that can be done in drilling on them is to highlight each one in turn and focus attention selectively on first one point, then another.

1.1 STRESS

Since accent marks are not written over the letters in English spelling, one might possibly think that stress is not important in English, or that a speaker may accent whatever syllables he happens to feel are the important ones. But such is not the case. Notice the pronunciation of the following:

Thĕ Whíte Hoùse (i.e., the President's residence)
Thĕ whíte hoúse (i.e., a house painted white)
Thĕ Whíte hoûse (i.e., a house owned by Mr. White)

A famous sentence to illustrate these differences is this:

Êverỹ whíte hoúse ìsn't thĕ Whíte Hoùse.

Another famous pair of examples is found in this sentence, where the importance of stress in English is obvious:

8

Lòng Íslănd ĭs ă lông íslănd.

For purposes of learning Spanish it does not especially matter whether one can hear exactly how many stresses there are in English or not. As a matter of fact, there are four clearly different degrees of prominence, marked in the examples above with four different kinds of accents:

- ⸍ strongest (also called primary or maximum or phrase stress)
- ⌢ strong (also called secondary or major or word stress)
- ⸌ medial (also called tertiary or minor)
- ⸜ weak (also called minimum or unstressed)

The only thing that matters for the present purpose is that we recognize that there <u>are</u> different degrees of prominence from one syllable to another and that these differences <u>mean</u> something. Recognizing this, we may examine the stress differences that are important in Spanish.

1.11 MINIMAL CONTRASTS

In Spanish there are normally only two degrees of stress. These are called <u>strong</u>, marked by an accent /′/ in the respelling of examples here, and <u>weak</u>, marked by a dot /·/ in the examples. The level of pitch of each syllable will later be indicated by placing the accent and the dot at different heights above the vowels, but for the purpose of focusing attention at first only on differences in prominence, the accents and dots are marked directly over the vowels.

The two columns below show <u>minimal stress contrasts</u>. They are paired words which differ only in the order in which the strong and weak stresses occur; the pitch of the syllables is partially conditioned by the stresses. In all other respects—vowels, consonants, junctures—they are identical. Yet the minimal stress differences (which are also minimal pitch differences) result in totally different meanings.

A			B		
Pronunciation	Spelling	Translation	Pronunciation	Spelling	Translation
éstà	esta	this	èstá	está	is
pápà	papa	potato	pàpá	papá	dad
pésò	peso	unit of money	pèsó	pesó	he weighed
píkò	pico	peak	pìkó	picó	he stung
íŋglès	ingles	groins	ìŋglés	inglés	English
líbrò	libro	book	lìbró	libró	he freed
árà	ara	altar	àrá	hará	he will do
ábrà	abra	open	àbrá	habrá	there will be
bérà	bera	edge	bèrá	verá	he will see
búrò	buro	chalk	bùró	buró	bureau
pérnò	perno	bolt	pèrnó	pernot	a kind of liquor

If a word has only one syllable, when it is pronounced in isolation it must have strong stress. But when it is in a phrase with at least one more syllable, it will sometimes have a strong stress and sometimes a weak stress. The result will be rhythmically the same as words which have two or more syllables. The place to begin with drill on stress, therefore, is with two- and three-syllable words. The words in the lists below have been selected to postpone introducing the especially difficult Spanish consonants and vowel sequences until after some mastery of stress has been achieved. In practicing the first drill, one should remember that it is as important to get the weak stresses right as it is to get the strong stresses right, since the English speaker will tend to make the weak stresses too weak.

1.12 TWO-SYLLABLE STRESS PATTERNS

Instructions.—Repeat after your model, working down each column of identical stress patterns. Cover the spelling.

	Pronunciation	Spelling		Pronunciation	Spelling
1	fúmò	fumo	1	èstá	está
2	téŋgà	tenga	2	ùstéd	usted
3	múchò	mucho	3	tàmbyén	también
4	gústò	gusto	4	dèşir	decir
5	nóchè	noche	5	pàsár	pasar
6	tántò	tanto	6	bìsté	bistec
7	bwénò	bueno	7	kàlór	calor
8	ástà	hasta	8	kàntó	cantó
9	dóndè	donde	9	pìkó	picó
10	pálò	palo	10	èstóy	estoy
11	básò	vaso	11	sàkó	sacó
12	kámà	cama	12	nàtál	natal
13	gótà	gota	13	bàyló	bailó
14	bámòs	vamos	14	chòkó	chocó
15	sólò	solo	15	fùmó	fumó
16	díchò	dicho	16	màmá	mamá
17	sákò	saco	17	pàpá	papá
18	pásò	paso	18	ìŋglés	inglés
19	sépà	sepa	19	kìtó	quitó
20	átò	hato	20	èsté	esté

1.13 THREE-SYLLABLE STRESS PATTERNS

Instructions.—Repeat after your model, working down each column of identical stress patterns. Cover the spelling.

Pronunciation ´ ◦ ◦	Spelling		Pronunciation ◦ ´ ◦	Spelling		Pronunciation ◦ ◦ ´	Spelling
1 lástìmà	lástima	1	èskúchè	escuche	1	èntèndí	entendí
2 únìkò	único	2	dìfíşìl	difícil	2	sàtànás	satanás
3 şéntìmò	céntimo	3	mòléstà	molesta	3	kònòşí	conocí
4 syéntèsè	siéntese	4	bèntánà	ventana	4	kòmìté	comité
5 póngàsè	póngase	5	mìnútòs	minutos	5	kàpìtán	capitán
6 kántìkò	cántico	6	kàndélà	candela	6	kàmìnó	caminó
7 káspìtà	cáspita	7	pàlítò	palito	7	mìlànés	milanés
8 tápàlò	tápalo	8	pòkítò	poquito	8	dòmìnó	dominó
9 kómìkò	cómico	9	èntónşès	entonces	9	dìspùté	disputé
10 démèlò	démelo	10	tàmpócò	tampoco	10	mòntànés	montanés
11 étìkò	ético	11	màntékà	manteca	11	ènèkén	henequén
12 élìşè	hélice	12	kàmínò	camino	12	òlàndés	holandés
13 ópèrà	ópera	13	kùlékà	culeca	13	màchùkó	machucó
14 mátàlà	mátala	14	kàmpánà	campana	14	àsùstó	asustó
15 mákìnà	máquina	15	fàmósò	famoso	15	pàtìné	patiné
16 mélìkò	mélico	16	sèmánà	semana	16	pàtàkón	patacón
17 mínìmò	mínimo	17	mìmósò	mimoso	17	kìtàpón	quitapón
18 kímìkà	química	18	mòléstò	molesto	18	èstàşyón	estación
19 mímìkò	mímico	19	mùlétà	muleta	19	sènsàşyón	sensación
20 límìtè	límite	20	pèpítà	pepita	20	lùnàşyón	lunación

1.2 PITCH AND JUNCTURE

Suppose someone says a short English sentence like "He went home." The chances are that if the sentence is in answer to a simple question like "Where's Billy?" it will be pronounced with a pitch pattern which can be marked like this:

   He went home.

There will be three levels of pitch involved which could be indicated on a musical staff in this way:

   He went home.

If we call the lowest of these three pitches <u>level /1/</u>, the middle one can be <u>level /2/</u>, and the highest one <u>level /3/</u>. The pitch pattern of the sentence can then be rewritten as

2 2 3-1   He went home.

Since, however, the second occurrence of level 2 is just a repetition of the first one, we can eliminate it and say that the pitch pattern of the sentence "He went home" should be written simply /2 3 1/. Furthermore, we can say that the first of the three pitch levels in this sentence occurs on the first syllable, the second occurs along with the strongest stress (on "home"), and the third occurs at the end. Finally we notice that at the end of the sentence there is a kind of squeezing-off of the stream of speech. We can write this squeezing-off with an arrow pointing downward, thus:

/2   3   1 ↓/   He went home.

This same squeezing-off would be represented on a musical staff like this:

   He went home.

This notation, /2   3   1 ↓/, represents the most common intonation pattern used in simple declarative sentences in English such as "He went home."

But suppose the question, instead of being "Where's Billy?" was something like "Did you say Billy went to the movies?" Then the answer would possibly be, "No, he went home." But now the pitch level on "home" is no longer level /3/; it is a step higher, and we can call it <u>level /4/</u>. This gives us a second basic pitch pattern of English:

/2   4   1 ↓/   He went <u>home</u>.

Finally, suppose that when the information that Billy went home is given, someone is surprised by this piece of news and indicates his surprise by the sentence: "He went home?" A third pitch pattern now appears which can be marked like this:

   He went home?

On a musical staff it might look like this:

   He went home?

It appears that the syllable "home," which starts out on level /3/, does not rise all the way to the next pitch level, so that a way to mark it is to use an arrow pointing upward, which indicates a rise in pitch after the last pitch level. It can then be written this way:

/2   3   3 ↑/   He went home.

We then have the same sentence spoken with three different pitch patterns resulting in three different meanings:

```
2        31
He went home↓        (simple statement)

2        41
He went home↓        (emphatic statement)

2        33
He went home↑        (echo question)
```

It is of course obvious that there are a great many pitch patterns in English besides these three, though not nearly so many as one might perhaps think; there are approximately fifty. The above three are very common ones; they will provide our first approximation toward a basis for comparison with Spanish.

In Spanish the pitch pattern which corresponds in frequency and meaning to the English pattern /2 3 1 ↓/ is a pattern which can be written /1 2 1 1 ↓/. This pattern can be taken as the uncolored base-line pattern with which all other patterns may be compared. The first number represents the pitch level of the first syllable. The second number represents the pitch level of the first syllable with strong stress, and the third number represents the pitch level of the second syllable with strong stress. The last number represents the pitch level of the last syllable. The pattern may vary greatly in the number of syllables that occur within it, but the examples and drills given here for mastering it show in most cases a simple alternation between weak and strong stress. The complex variations possible in this pattern, and many other patterns, will be taken up after the details of vowels and consonants have been examined.

Some people find that the use of numbers to represent pitch levels is confusing. Therefore the pitch levels in Spanish will be indicated by the <u>height</u> of the dots and accents that have already been used to mark stresses. One can then make a direct equation between height of pitch and height of dots or accents above vowels. It is a little like following the bouncing ball that movies use to lead group singing. Illustrations of the several possible ways of marking stress, pitch, and juncture are shown below. The first is the one that will be used in the drills. The sentence is "Comemos mucho."

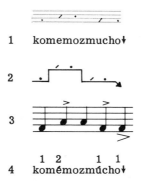

```
1    komemozmucho↓

2    

3    

     1 2    1 1
4    komémozmúcho↓
```

The first problem is simply to get this pattern in mind, since it is different from the English pattern /2 3 1 ↓/ with which it must be compared in distribution and meaning. To that end the following drill is directed. As with the drills on stress, most of the difficult problems with consonants have been carefully avoided, so that attention may be focused almost entirely on the intonation pattern.

1.21 NORMAL STATEMENT PATTERN /1 2 1 1 ↓/

Instructions.—Repeat after your model, working down the column and associating the rise and fall of pitch with the height of dots and accents. Cover the spelling.

Pronunciation	Spelling	Pronunciation	Spelling
/1 2 1 1 ↓/			
1 komemozmucho↓	Comemos mucho.	11 fumandopipas↓	Fumando pipas.
2 estakasado↓	Está casado.	12 estakontento↓	Está contento.
3 estudyampoko↓	Estudian poco.	13 sekandokosas↓	Secando cosas.
4 empyesapako↓	Empieza Paco.	14 komyendotakos↓	Comiendo tacos.
5 tomamoskopa↓	Tomamos copa.	15 pelandopapas↓	Pelando papas.
6 paketetengo↓	Paquete tengo.	16 maskandokoka↓	Mascando coca.
7 komistepapas↓	Comiste papas.	17 amamozmucho↓	Amamos mucho.
8 mariatoka↓	Mariá toca.	18 muchachospobres↓	Muchachos pobres.
9 tomasipepe↓	Tomás y Pepe	19 nityenesako↓	Ni tiene saco.
10 estasechando↓	Estás echando.	20 insistemucho↓	Insiste mucho.

With the normal statement pattern in mind, it is possible to make the first set of comparisons. We have already noted that the simple, uncolored statement pattern in

English is /2 3 1 ↓/. The pattern which <u>sounds</u> most like this in Spanish /1 2 3 1↓/, but this pattern, rather than being a simple statement pattern, is strongly emphatic in Spanish, comparable in meaning to the English pattern /2 4 1 ↓/. The following exercise consists of changing the now familiar Spanish pattern /1 2 1 1↓/ to the emphatic pattern /1 2 3 1↓/. As you make the changes, try to associate the meaning of special emphasis that properly belongs with the latter pattern, because your tendency, as a speaker of English for whom this pattern is quite neutral, will be to think of this pattern as normal or colorless. But at the same time be very careful not to make the emphatic pitch level /3/ go too high, since you will tend to make it like your own pitch level /4/ in the emphatic English pattern.

1.22 EMPHATIC STATEMENT PATTERN /1 2 3 1 ↓/

<u>Instructions.</u>—Mimic your model's pronunciation of the utterances in the first column. Then repeat each utterance, replacing the normal pattern with the emphatic pattern shown in the second column. Cover the spelling.

Pronunciation		Spelling
Normal /1 2 1 1 ↓/	Emphatic /1 2 3 1 ↓/	
1 komemozmucho↓	komemozmucho↓	Comemos mucho.
2 maŋyanabeŋgo↓	maŋyanabeŋgo↓	Mañana vengo.
3 tampokopasa↓	tampokopasa↓	Tampoco pasa.
4 kaminapoko↓	kaminapoko↓	Camina poco.
5 molestatanta↓	molestatanto↓	Molesta tanto.
6 bendimikama↓	bendimikama↓	Vendí mi cama.
7 tenemosocho↓	tenemosocho↓	Tenemos ocho.
8 komistepapas↓	komistepapas↓	Comiste papas.

Pronunciation		Spelling
Normal /1 2 1 1 ↓/	Emphatic /1 2 3 1 ↓/	
9 estakontento↓	estakontento↓	Está contento.
10 maskandokoka↓	maskandokoka↓	Mascando coca.
11 isoydechile↓	isoydechile↓	Y soy de Chile.
12 estaokupado↓	estaokupado↓	Está ocupado.
13 pronunsyastodo↓	pronunsyastodo↓	Pronuncias todo.
14 buskamoskasa↓	buskamoskasa↓	Buscamos casa.
15 estudyampoko↓	estudyampoko↓	Estudian poco.
16 ibyenenmuchos↓	ibyenenmuchos↓	Y vienen muchos
17 pelandopapas↓	pelandopapas↓	Pelando papas.
18 komyendotakos↓	komyendotakos↓	Comiendo tacos.
19 amamozmucho↓	amamozmucho↓	Amamos mucho.
20 insistemucho↓	insistemucho↓	Insiste mucho.

A good many people, when they see a question mark at the end of a sentence, think it must mean that the pitch of the voice is supposed to rise. This is a strange misapprehension, and it is found both among English speakers and among Spanish speakers.

When a question begins with a question word—who, what, which, why, etc.—in either language, the intonation pattern that occurs is identical with the normal uncolored statement pattern unless, again, there is special emphasis present. Thus "When did he go?" has the same intonation as "I went yesterday." The question marks used in traditional orthography do not indicate anything about the intonation in such questions and are potentially misleading. Questions which begin with question words may be called information questions; they occur in two patterns, normal and emphatic, just like the two statement patterns that were drilled above. In the following practice, you are again cautioned to keep pitch level /3/ down: you will tend to make it too high.

1.23 INFORMATION QUESTION PATTERNS
/1211↓/ VS. /1231↓/

Instructions.—Mimic your model's pronunciation of the utterances in the first column. Then repeat each utterance, replacing the normal pattern with the emphatic pattern shown in the second column. Cover the spelling.

Pronunciation		Spelling
Normal /1 2 1 1 ↓/	Emphatic /1 2 3 1 ↓/	
1 ikwantopoŋgo↓	ikwantopoŋgo↓	¿Y cuánto pongo?
2 ikwandobeŋgo↓	ikwandobeŋgo↓	¿Y cuándo vengo?
3 porkemolestas↓	porkemolestas↓	¿Por qué molestas?
4 iketomamos↓	iketomamos↓	¿Y qué tomamos?
5 ikwandokomen↓	ikwandokomen↓	¿Y cuándo comen?
6 ikwandofuman↓	ikwandofuman↓	¿Y cuándo fuman?
7 endondekeda↓	endondekeda↓	¿En dónde queda?
8 deketamaɲyo↓	deketamaɲyo↓	¿De qué tamaño?

Pronunciation		Spelling
Normal /1 2 1 1 ↓/	Emphatic /1 2 3 1 ↓/	
9 porkesepegan↓	porkesepegan↓	¿Por qué se pegan?
10 ikwantopesan↓	ikwantopesan↓	¿Y cuánto pesan?
11 adondefwiste↓	adondefwiste↓	¿Adónde fuiste?
12 dedondebyenen↓	dedondebyenen↓	¿De dónde vienen?
13 idondekomen↓	idondekomen↓	¿Y dónde comen?
14 paraketrabahamos↓	paraketrabahamos↓	¿Para qué trabajamos?
15 idondelozmandas↓	idondelozmandas↓	¿Y dónde los mandas?
16 ikomolokyeres↓	ikomolokyeres↓	¿Y cómo lo quieres?
17 ikwandoloalkilan↓	ikwandoloalkilan↓	¿Y cuándo lo alquilan?
18 ikwandolobemos↓	ikwandolobemos↓	¿Y cuándo lo vemos?
19 porkeselodise↓	porkeselodise↓	¿Por qué se lo dice?
20 ikwandosalimos↓	ikwandosalimos↓	¿Y cuándo salimos?

The other common type of question is the one that can be answered with a simple yes or no. This kind of question never begins with a question word; and while it often has a special word-order in either English or Spanish, it may differ from a statement only by having a different intonation but no special word-order whatever. The typical yes-no question intonation in English is /2 3 3 ↑/. The rise in pitch which is marked by /↑/ may be rather leisurely in English and have considerable spread from the level on which it begins to its end. The comparable Spanish intonation pattern is /1 2 2 2 ↑/. The rise marked by the arrow in Spanish indicates a rise which is actually faster than the English rise, more abrupt, and lacking in the noticeable spread of the English rise. When you listen to these questions, note that while the final dot above the last weak-stressed syllable of each pattern is placed on a level with the preceding accent, the last syllable is always higher in pitch than the dot shows—a fact which is signaled by the arrow. In the following practice, you are cautioned to keep the end-rise short and abrupt; this is perfectly well-mannered in Spanish, even though in English it would sound rather brusque.

1.24 YES-NO QUESTION PATTERN /1222↑/

Instructions.—Mimic your model's pronunciation of the utterances in the first column. Then repeat each utterance, replacing the normal statement pattern with the yes-no question pattern shown in the second column. Cover the spelling.

Pronunciation		Spelling
Normal statement /1 2 1 1 ↓/	Yes-no question /1 2 2 2 ↑/	
1 komistepapas↓	komistepapas↑	(¿)Comiste papas(?)
2 fumandopipa↓	fumandopipa↑	(¿)Fumando pipa(?)
3 komyendotakos↓	komyendotakos↑	(¿)Comiendo tacos(?)
4 nityenesako↓	nityenesako↑	(¿)Ni tiene saco(?)
5 sekandokosas↓	sekandokosas↑	(¿)Secando cosas(?)
6 isombonitas↓	isombonitas↑	(¿)Y son bonitas(?)
7 estudyampoko↓	estudyampoko↑	(¿)Estudian poco(?)

Pronunciation		Spelling
Normal statement /1 2 1 1 ↓/	Yes-no question /1 2 2̌ 2 ↑/	
8 estakansado↓	estakansado↑	(¿)Está cansado(?)
9 sebendenawtos↓	sebendenawtos↑	(¿)Se venden autos(?)
10 deseanalgo↓	deseanalgo↑	(¿)Desean algo(?)
11 legustaelpresyo↓	legustaelpresyo↑	(¿)Le gusta el precio(?)
12 buskamosotro↓	buskamosotro↑	(¿)Buscamos otro(?)
13 kompramossabanas↓	kompramossabanas↑	(¿)Compramos sábanas(?)
14 subimoshuntos↓	subimoshuntos↑	(¿)Subimos juntos(?)
15 trabahanmucho↓	trabahanmucho↑	(¿)Trabajan mucho(?)
16 alkilaelkwarto↓	alkilaelkwarto↑	(¿)Alquila el cuarto(?)
17 tomamosuntaksi↓	tomamosuntaksi↑	(¿)Tomamos un taxi(?)
18 almorsamoshuntos↓	almorsamoshuntos↑	(¿)Almorzamos juntos(?)
19 leparesemucho↓	leparesemucho↑	(¿)Le parece mucho(?)
20 legustalanoche↓	legustalanoche↑	(¿)Le gusta la noche(?)

One final pattern of high frequency will provide enough of an introduction to Spanish intonation to make it worthwhile to go on and look into the details of the vowels and consonants which carry the intonation. This pattern, in contrast with the yes-no pattern, can be called simply the yes question pattern, since the person to whom it is addressed is expected to agree and the question would not be uttered with this intonation unless agreement were expected; in fact, the expectation of agreement is so strong that the questioner is often nodding his head as he asks the question, or at least his eyebrows are raised in anticipation. It is presented last of the four basic patterns we are starting out from—the first three being /1 2 1 1 ↓/, /1 2 3 1 ↓/, and /1 2 2 2 ↑/—because the most nearly similar English pattern is quite rare, making this one the most difficult of these four Spanish patterns for the student to learn. It can be symbolized as /1 2 3 1 |/. It differs from the emphatic pattern, /1 2 3 1 ↓/, only in the way it ends. The downward arrow of the emphatic pattern symbolizes a quick drop-off in pitch accompanied by a fade-out of intensity. The single bar of the yes question signals no drop-off in pitch beyond the last pitch level, and instead of a fade-out of intensity, it signals a rather sharp cut-off without fade. While this difference seems small when one talks about it or tries to describe it, it is easy to hear.

1.25 YES QUESTION PATTERN /1 2 3 1 |/

Instructions.—Mimic your model's pronunciation of the utterances in the first column. Then repeat each utterance, replacing the yes-no question pattern with the yes question pattern shown in the second column.

Pronunciation		Spelling
Yes-no question /1 2 2 2 ↑/	Yes question /1 2 3 1 |/	
1 estakontento↑	estakontento|	¿ Está contento?
2 tomamoskopa↑	tomamoskopa|	¿ Tomamos copa?
3 empyeşapako↑	empyeşapako|	¿ Empieza Paco?
4 estasechando↑	estasechando|	¿ Estás echando?
5 estaneŋkasa↑	estaneŋkasa|	¿ Están en casa?

Pronunciation		Spelling
Yes-no question /1 2 2 2 ↑/	Yes question /1 2 3 1 ↓/	
6 niesokiso↑	niesokiso↓	¿Ni eso quiso?
7 estamfumando↑	estamfumando↓	¿Están fumando?
8 estaenlakosta↑	estaenlakosta↓	¿Está en la costa?
9 legustalasopa↑	legustalasopa↓	¿Le gusta la sopa?
10 ityenesita↑	ityenesita↓	¿Y tiene cita?
11 kaminamucho↑	kaminamucho↓	¿Camina mucho?
12 tampokobyenes↑	tampokobyenes↓	¿Tampoco vienes?
13 komistetakos↑	komistetakos↓	¿Comiste tacos?
14 sekitoelsako↑	sekitoelsako↓	¿Se quitó el saco?
15 legustalakasa↑	legustalakasa↓	¿Le gusta la casa?
16 leparesebastante↑	leparesebastante↓	¿Le parece bastante?
17 tampokotrabahas↑	tampokotrabahas↓	¿Tampoco trabajas?
18 todabiahuntos↑	todabiahuntos↓	¿Todavía juntos?

Pronunciation		Spelling
Yes-no question /1 2 2 2 ↓/	Yes question /1 2 3 1 |/	
19 neṣesitalmọaḍas↑	neṣesitalmọaḍas|	¿Necesita almohadas?
20 estalabwelta↑	estalabwelta|	¿Está a la vuelta?

The only difference between the sequences in Drill 1.26 uttered as yes questions and uttered as emphatic statements is in the way they end: /|/ for yes questions and /↓/ for emphatic statements. The rest of the pattern is identical, and this small difference is worth drilling on.

1.26 YES QUESTIONS VS. EMPHATIC STATEMENTS

Instructions.—Mimic your model's pronunciation of the utterances in the first column. Then repeat each utterance, replacing the yes question pattern with the emphatic statement pattern shown in the second column. Note that the sharp cut-off of the final /|/ of the yes questions is replaced by the lower drop and gradual fade-out of the final /↓/.

Pronunciation		Spelling
Yes question /1 2 3 1 |/	Emphatic statement /1 2 3 1 ↓/	
1 estakontento|	estakontento↓	(¿)Está contento(?)
2 tomamoskopa|	tomamoskopa↓	(¿)Tomamos copa(?)
3 empyeṣapako|	empyeṣapako↓	(¿)Empieza Paco(?)
4 estasechando|	estasechando↓	(¿)Estás echando(?)
5 estaneŋkasa|	estaneŋkasa↓	(¿)Están en casa(?)

Pronunciation		Spelling
Yes question /1 2 3 1 /	Emphatic statement /1 2 3 1 /	
6 niesokiso|	niesokiso	(¿)Ni eso quiso(?)
7 estamfumando|	estamfumando	(¿)Están fumando(?)
8 estaẹnlakosta|	estaẹnlakosta	(¿)Está en la costa(?)
9 legustalasopa|	legustalasopa	(¿)Le gusta la sopa(?)
10 ityeneṣita|	ityeneṣita	(¿)Y tiene cita(?)
11 kaminamucho|	kaminamucho	(¿)Camina mucho(?)
12 tampokobyenes|	tampokobyenes	(¿)Tampoco vienes(?)
13 komistetakos|	komistetakos	(¿)Comiste tacos(?)
14 sekitoẹlsako|	sekitoẹlsako	(¿)Se quitó el saco(?)
15 legustalakasa|	legustalakasa	(¿)Le gusta la casa(?)
16 lepareṣebastante|	lepareṣebastante	(¿)Le parece bastante(?)
17 tampokotrabahas|	tampokotrabahas	(¿)Tampoco trabajas(?)
18 todabiahuntos|	todabiahuntos	(¿)Todavía juntos(?)

Pronunciation		Spelling
Yes question /1 2 3 1 |/	Emphatic statement /1 2 3 1 ↓/	
19 nesesitalmoadas|	nesesitalmoadas↓	( )Necesita almohadas(?)
20 estalabwelta|	estalabwelta↓	( )Está a la vuelta(?)

1.3 | RHYTHM

Rhythm is not itself an element of intonation, but it <u>does</u> have important and very noticeable consequences on the quality of one's pronunciation. Rhythm is created in language by two elements: (1) length of syllables; (2) number of syllables per unit of time, i.e., rate. In Spanish, the length of syllables is relatively constant. Commonplace names will serve to illustrate the difference, with syllable length shown underneath by dots, each representing a minimum unit of length (thus .. is twice as long as .):

English Pronunciation	Spanish Pronunciation
Perú	Perú
Havana	Habana
Buenos Aires	Buenos Aires
Santiago	Santiago
Tegucigalpa	Tegucigalpa
Managua, Nicaragua	Managua, Nicaragua

Since the length of syllables is relatively constant in Spanish—all syllables are either one unit long or two units long, depending in general on whether the syllable has weak or strong stress—the number of syllables per unit of time is almost constant. The acoustic effect of this constancy in rate on the English ear is an effect of machine-gun-like rapidity and regularity. The American is immediately convinced that Spanish is spoken at an unreasonably rapid rate, which he can never hope to master. The fact is quite otherwise, however; it is the American who is likely to speak at the faster rate, if his speech is measured in the same way, because his syllables under weak stress are noticeably shorter than any Spanish syllable and because his tendency is to skip very rapidly over the short syllables and prolong the longer (heavier-stressed) syllables substantially beyond the duration of any Spanish syllable. Compare the following words, which are identical in number of syllables:

rẹspọnsịbị̣lị̣ty	rẹspọnsạbị̣lịdạd
ọblig̣ạtiọn	ọbligạciọ́n
nọtạtiọn	nọtạciọ́n
cọncẹptiọn	cọncẹpciọ́n

Note that the strong syllables of English are noticeably longer than those of Spanish—and the weak syllables are noticeably shorter. This difference has been characterized as the difference between a <u>stress</u>-<u>timed</u> language (English tends to require a certain regularity in the rate of recurrence of strong stresses) and a <u>syllable</u>-<u>timed</u> language (Spanish tends to require a certain regularity in the rate of recurrence of syllables, regardless of length). The difference has been, perhaps, exaggerated, although there can be no doubt that the essential fact is important, namely, that Spanish syllable structure admits of relatively slight variation in length and rate, while English syllable structure demands very substantial variation on both counts.

All the examples and exercises up to this point can now be reviewed with the facts about rhythm in mind.

1.4 | BEYOND THE ELEMENTS OF INTONATION

Intonation is rather more complex than this description and set of drills have perhaps made it appear. Some of the additional complexities are these:

1. The number of syllables within a single pattern varies greatly. All the examples so far have been rigorously controlled as to the number of syllables and sequence of alternation between strong and weak stress.
2. The different intonation patterns, including many more besides the four very common ones, combine with each other in a variety of complex ways.
3. Intonation patterns occur along with all the sounds of the language, not merely with the restricted inventory of the easier sounds (for English speakers) utilized in constructing the preceding drills.
4. Any given intonation pattern may be overlaid by the addition of what may be called <u>vocalizations</u>, which include phenomena like overloudness and oversoftness, overhigh pitch and overlow pitch, rasp, tonelessness, and a number of other additive features which are not themselves part of the intonation patterns but which modify, intensify, heighten, and otherwise support the intonation patterns themselves.

The total complexity of all the facts which taken together are called <u>intonation</u> is not by any means beyond the possibility of mastery with very nearly the same degree of accuracy with which the vowels and consonants can be dominated. With the basis for practice on intonation provided by the preceding drills, we will now go on to the details of vowels and consonants and afterward return to pull together all aspects of the sound system of Spanish, including practice on more complex intonation patterns.

THE VOWELS 2

One of the first problems one faces in any new language is to determine how many different vowels there are. It is unlikely that there will be any real agreement between that number and the number of symbols there are in the alphabet for representing the vowels. Thus in English all vowels have to be written with six letters—a e i o u y —and yet English has, depending on dialect, between seven and ten simple vowels and up to twenty-seven complex vowels, or diphthongs. To determine how many really different vowels there are, it is necessary to seek out groups of words which have the same consonants but are different words because of the vowels. Thus in English one might draw up a list of words like "sit, set, sat, Sutt, sot, soot, sought"; or one like "sea, say, sigh, soy, sow, sew, sue"; and there would be still others not like any of these. It is not necessary to go into the details of English vowels, but it is important to recognize that it is not letters of the alphabet we are talking about.

2.0 | MINIMAL CONTRASTS—VOWELS

Word lists like the English samples above are especially easy to construct in Spanish: there are only five vowels in Spanish. The orthography keeps these vowels nicely distinct with five letters, a e i o u; the spelling falls down only in the slight overlap where y can represent the same sound as i and in the fact that four of these symbols can also represent certain consonant-like sounds. A sample word list of the type one must construct in order to learn about vowel contrasts is cited below. It is not intended as a drill primarily but rather as an illustration of minimal contrasts.

Illustration of Vowel Contrasts				
/i/	/e/	/a/	/o/	/u/

1 tí
    ti
	té
	  té
		tá
		  ta
			tó
			  to
				tú
				  tú

2 sí
    sí
	sé
	  sé
		s̨á
		  za
			só
			  so
				sú
				  su

3 bís
    bis
	bés
	  ves
		bás
		  vas
			bós
			  vos
				bús
				  bus

4 písȯ
    piso
	pésȯ
	  peso
		pásȯ
		  paso
			pósȯ
			  poso
				púsȯ
				  puso

27

Illustration of Vowel Contrasts				
/i/	/e/	/a/	/o/	/u/

	/i/	/e/	/a/	/o/	/u/
5	límă Lima	lémă lema	lámă lama	lómă loma	lúmă luma
6	pípă pipa	pépă pepa	pápă papa	pópă popa	púpă pupa
7	kínă quina	kénă quena	kánă cana	kónă cona	kúnă cuna
8	píkŏ pico	pékŏ peco	pákŏ paco	pókŏ poco	púkŏ puco
9	tílă tila	télă tela	tálă tala	tólă tola	túlă Tula
10	pílŏ pilo	pélŏ pelo	pálŏ palo	pólŏ polo	púlŏ pulo
11	kísŏ quiso	késŏ queso	kásŏ caso	kósŏ coso	kúsŏ cuso
12	bígă viga	bégă vega	bágă vaga	bógă boga	búgă Buga
13	íƀă iba	éƀă Eva	áƀă haba	óƀă ova	úƀă uva
14	híră gira	héră jera	háră jara	hóră jora	húră jura
15	hítă jita	hétă jeta	hátă jata	hótă jota	hútă juta

2.1 | WEAK-STRESSED VOWELS

If one were to single out the most persistent difficulty encountered by English speakers learning Spanish, he might well suggest that it results from the fact that all five Spanish vowels occur with great frequency <u>under</u> <u>weak</u> <u>stress</u> <u>without</u> <u>any</u> <u>significant</u> <u>change</u> <u>of</u> <u>phonetic</u> <u>quality</u> <u>from</u> <u>the</u> <u>strong-stressed</u> <u>phonetic</u> <u>shape</u>, whereas in English all vowels can occur under one of the strong stresses <u>but</u> <u>only</u> <u>certain</u> <u>ones</u> <u>occur</u> <u>with</u> <u>any</u> <u>regularity</u> <u>under</u> <u>weak</u> stress.

This limitation on vowels under weak stress in English can be seen by comparing normal pronunciation of the word "is" in these two sentences:

      (a) Ìs Rôse gǒíng?
      (b) Rôse ĭs gǒíng.

The stress levels are marked for those who remember what was said about them in the discussion of intonation, but <u>any</u> normal reading of these sentences which gives loudest stress to the last word will show a difference between the vowel of "is" in (a) and the vowel of "is" in (b). To refer to them, we will use the symbols /i/ "eye" and /ɨ/ "barred-eye." /ɨ/ is the vowel that occurs most frequently in English syllables that are under weak stress. /ɨ/ is the vowel produced with the tongue in the middle of the mouth in its most relaxed position. The underlined letters of the following words are all pronounced with /ɨ/: Dall<u>a</u>s, Dull<u>e</u>s, thes<u>i</u>s, En<u>o</u>s, min<u>u</u>s, sof<u>a</u>, bubbl<u>e</u>, nick<u>e</u>l, pris<u>o</u>n, pris<u>m</u>, heat<u>e</u>d, <u>a</u>bout, <u>o</u>ccur, <u>u</u>ntil, an<u>i</u>mal, miner<u>a</u>l. The vowel /ɨ/ is the most frequently occurring of English sounds, and the fact that it occurs with great regularity in English in weak-stressed syllables makes it probable that it will be carried over into Spanish by English speaking students. <u>But this sound is not even in the inventory of Spanish sounds</u>; the whole problem with weak-stressed syllables in Spanish is that /ɨ/ does not occur in them, whereas vowels like /a/ and /e/ and /o/ occur regularly in weak-stressed syllables and with great frequency. One would think this ought not to be so great a problem, but the habitual patterns of English carry over forcefully, usually entirely without the English speaker's even being aware that he is not making an /a/ or an /e/ and entirely without his being aware that he is in fact substituting /ɨ/.

The drills which follow here are designed to do something about this serious difficulty. In these lists nearly every vowel transcribed with a dot over it is likely to be pronounced by an English speaker as /ɨ/, which does not exist in Spanish. Reduction of any of the Spanish vowels will result in loss of contrast between the minimally different items of the two columns: that is, words which ought to sound different will be pronounced as though they sounded alike, and potential misunderstanding is the consequence.

2.11 WEAK-STRESSED VOWEL CONTRASTS

Instructions.—Mimic your model's pronunciation of these items in pairs. Try to say each one of the pair exactly alike except for the minimal vowel difference: that is, use exactly the same intonation and stress pattern for each item. Cover the spelling.

2.11.1 DRILL ON /ă/ VS. /ĕ/

	Pronunciation		Spelling	
	/ă/	/ĕ/		
1	pȧnál	pėnál	panal	penal
2	mȧnár	mėnár	manar	menar
3	pȧŋyól	pėŋyól	pañol	peñol
4	bȧsár	bėsár	basar	besar
5	pȧlón	pėlón	palón	pelón
6	mȧchón	mėchón	machón	mechón
7	fȧtál	fėtál	fatal	fetal
8	ȧpȧgár	ȧpėgár	apagar	apegar
9	mȧsítȧ	mėsítȧ	masita	mesita
10	kȧsérȧ	kėsérȧ	casera	quesera
11	bȧládȧ	bėládȧ	balada	velada
12	pȧpítȧ	pėpítȧ	papita	pepita
13	frȧŋȿésȧs	frȧŋȿésės	francesas	franceses

Pronunciation		Spelling	
/ă/	/ĕ/		
14 sènyóràs	sènyórès	señoras	señores
15 àpénàs	àpénès	apenas	apenes
16 mésàs	mésès	mesas	meses
17 látàn	látèn	latan	laten
18 kítàn	kítèn	quitan	quiten
19 bátàn	bátèn	batan	baten
20 kéḋàn	kéḋèn	quedan	queden

2.11.2 DRILL ON /ă/ VS. /ĭ/

/ă/	/ĭ/		
1 pànyál	pìnyál	pañal	piñal
2 pànṣón	pìnṣón	panzón	pinzón
3 mátáḋ	mìtáḋ	matad	mitad
4 kàtár	kìtár	catar	quitar
5 pàtón	pìtón	patón	pitón
6 nàḋár	nìḋár	nadar	nidar
7 làḃár	lìḃár	lavar	libar
8 chàrlár	chìrlár	charlar	chirlar
9 mà(l)yàḋór	mà(l)yìḋór	mallador	mallidor
10 pàsándò	pìsándò	pasando	pisando
11 màsítà	mìsítà	masita	misita
12 sàlérò	sìlérò	salero	silero
13 fàháròn	fìháròn	fajaron	fijaron
14 làtérà	lìtérà	latera	litera
15 pàkétè	pìkétè	paquete	piquete
16 bàsáḋà	bìsáḋà	basada	visada
17 bàsítà	bìsítà	basita	visita
18 kúrsà	kúrsì	cursa	cursi
19 hílà	hílì	Gila	Gili
20 kásà	kásì	casa	casi

2.11.3 DRILL ON /ă/ VS. /ŏ/

/ă/	/ŏ/		
1 pàsyón	pòsyón	pasión	poción
2 màlár	mòlár	malar	molar
3 pàpél	pòpél	papel	popel
4 kàlór	kòlór	calor	color
5 kàsíta	kòsíta	casita	cosita
6 pàsáḋà	pòsáḋà	pasada	posada

Pronunciation		Spelling	
/ă/	/ŏ/		
7 păstí(l)yă	pŏstí(l)yă	pastilla	postilla
8 păsárŏn	pŏsárŏn	pasaron	posaron
9 trăŋkítă	trŏŋkítă	tranquita	tronquita
10 păkítŏ	pŏkítŏ	Paquito	poquito
11 pătáhĕ	pŏtáhĕ	pataje	potaje
12 păténtĕ	pŏténtĕ	patente	potente
13 păléă	pŏléă	palea	polea
14 pămpítă	pŏmpítă	pampita	pompita
15 pătérnă	pŏtérnă	paterna	poterna
16 băládă	bŏládă	balada	bolada
17 măríă	mŏríă	María	moría
18 ĕrmánăs	ĕrmánŏs	hermanas	hermanos
19 mĭmósăs	mĭmósŏs	mimosas	mimosos
20 pésăs	pésŏs	pesas	pesos

2.11.4 DRILL ON /ă/ VS. /ŭ/

/ă/	/ŭ/		
1 găstár	gŭstár	gastar	gustar
2 ămór	ŭmór	amor	humor
3 păhár	pŭhár	pajar	pujar
4 tărón	tŭrón	tarón	turón
5 măsítă	mŭsítă	masita	musita
6 fămósŏ	fŭmósŏ	famoso	fumoso
7 lănítă	lŭnítă	lanita	lunita
8 kănítă	kŭnítă	canita	cunita
9 mălítă	mŭlítă	malita	mulita
10 mălásŏ	mŭlásŏ	malazo	mulazo
11 kăɲyádŏ	kŭɲyádŏ	cañado	cuñado
12 mărsyánŏ	mŭrsyánŏ	Marciano	Murciana
13 săbídŏ	sŭbídŏ	sabido	subido
14 păpítă	pŭpítă	papita	pupita
15 lănérŏ	lŭnérŏ	lanero	lunero
16 kărákăs	kŭrákăs	Caracas	curacas
17 părgítă	pŭrgítă	parguita	purguita
18 bărrítă	bŭrrítă	barrita	burrita
19 pălĭdés̠	pŭlĭdés̠	palidez	pulidez
20 mătădór	mŭtădór	matador	mutador

2.11.5 DRILL ON /ĕ/ VS. /ĭ/

	Pronunciation		Spelling	
	/ĕ/	/ĭ/		
1	pĕnár	pĭnár	penar	pinar
2	rrĕmár	rrĭmár	remar	rimar
3	pĕlón	pĭlón	pelón	pilón
4	tĕlón	tĭlón	telón	tilón
5	mĕ(l)yár	mĭ(l)yár	mellar	millar
6	pĕtón	pĭtón	petón	pitón
7	pĕké	pĭké	pequé	piqué
8	ĕnşéstŏ	ĭnşéstŏ	encesto	incesto
9	bĕşérrá	bĭşérrá	becerra	bicerra
10	dĕskántĕ	dĭskántĕ	descante	discante
11	sĕséŏ	sĭséŏ	seseo	siseo
12	pĕsádá	pĭsádá	pesada	pisada
13	pĕsárŏn	pĭsárŏn	pesaron	pisaron
14	mĕsérá	mĭsérá	mesera	misera
15	pĕsádŏ	pĭsádŏ	pesado	pisado
16	pĕŋyítá	pĭŋyítá	peñita	piñita
17	ĕmítĕ	ĭmítĕ	emite	imite
18	pĕrítá	pĭrítá	perita	pirita
19	hĕtádá	hĭtádá	jetada	jitada
20	chĕkítŏ	chĭkítŏ	chequito	chiquito

2.11.6 DRILL ON /ĕ/ VS. /ŏ/

	/ĕ/	/ŏ/		
1	lĕsyón	lŏsyón	lesión	losión
2	pĕlár	pŏlár	pelar	polar
3	mĕntón	mŏntón	mentón	montón
4	bĕráş	bŏráş	veraz	voraz
5	mĕsítá	mŏsítá	mesita	mosita
6	pĕsádŏ	pŏsádŏ	pesado	posado
7	sĕsérá	sŏsérá	sesera	sosera
8	tĕşádŏ	tŏşádŏ	tezado	tozado
9	pĕsárŏn	pŏsárŏn	pesaron	posaron
10	bĕlítá	bŏlítá	velita	bolita
11	ĕrmítá	ŏrmítá	ermita	hormita
12	tĕrnérŏ	tŏrnérŏ	ternero	tornero
13	gĕrrítá	gŏrrítá	guerrita	gorrita
14	şĕrrítŏ	şŏrrítŏ	cerrito	zorrito
15	bĕtádŏ	bŏtádŏ	betado	botado

Pronunciation		Spelling	
/ĕ/	/ŏ/		
16 ĕbádá	ŏbádá	evada	ovada
17 pásĕs	pásŏs	pases	pasos
18 kábĕs	kábŏs	cabes	cabos
19 tírĕs	tírŏs	tires	tiros
20 prĕpŏsísyón	prŏpŏsísyón	preposición	proposición

2.11.7 DRILL ON /ĕ/ VS. /ŭ/

/ĕ/	/ŭ/		
1 fĕstín	fŭstín	festín	fustín
2 pĕnsyón	pŭnsyón	pensión	punción
3 tĕmór	tŭmór	temor	tumor
4 pĕlgár	pŭlgár	pelgar	pulgar
5 lĕchár	lŭchár	lechar	luchar
6 lĕchón	lŭchón	lechón	luchón
7 sĕksyón	sŭksyón	sección	succión
8 lĕgár	lŭgár	legar	lugar
9 sĕrrár	sŭrrár	cerrar	zurrar
10 ásĕstár	ásŭstár	asestar	asustar
11 ánĕlár	ánŭlár	anelar	anular
12 mĕsítá	mŭsítá	mesita	musita
13 pĕnsádŏ	pŭnsádŏ	pensado	punzado
14 tĕndérŏ	tŭndérŏ	tendero	tundero
15 lĕlítŏ	lŭlítŏ	lelito	lulito
16 ádĕlántĕ	ádŭlántĕ	adelante	adulante
17 pĕchérŏ	pŭchérŏ	pechero	puchero
18 rrĕtíná	rrŭtíná	retina	rutina
19 pĕrítá	pŭrítá	perita	purita
20 sĕrkádŏ	sŭrkádŏ	cercado	surcado

2.11.8 DRILL ON /ĭ/ VS. /ŏ/

/ĭ/	/ŏ/		
1 lĭsár	lŏsár	lisar	losar
2 sĭsár	sŏsár	sisar	sosar
3 mĭsyón	mŏsyón	misión	moción
4 trĭŋkár	trŏŋkár	trincar	troncar
5 fĭgón	fŏgón	figón	fogón
6 tĭmó	tŏmó	timó	tomó
7 mĭrár	mŏrár	mirar	morar
8 mĭ(l)yár	mŏ(l)yár	millar	mollar

Pronunciation		Spelling	
/ĭ/	/ŏ/		
9 nĭḇél	nŏḇél	nivel	novel
10 nĭḇelár	nŏḇelár	nivelar	novelar
11 pĭsádá	pŏsádá	pisada	posada
12 ĭṣádá	ŏsádá	izada	osada
13 ĭmítŏ	ŏmítŏ	imito	omito
14 pĭkítŏ	pŏkítŏ	piquito	poquito
15 tĭrítŏ	tŏrítŏ	tirito	torito
16 mĭrádá	mŏrádá	mirada	morada
17 ĭhítŏ	ŏhítŏ	hijito	ojito
18 tĭntísĭmŏ	tŏntísĭmŏ	tintísimo	tontísimo
19 fĭgŏnérŏ	fŏgŏnérŏ	figonero	fogonero
20 múhĭl	múhŏl	múgil	mújol

2.11.9 DRILL ON /ĭ/ VS. /ŭ/

/ĭ/	/ŭ/		
1 fĭsyón	fŭsyón	fisión	fusión
2 pĭntár	pŭntár	pintar	puntar
3 pĭnṣón	pŭnṣón	pinzón	punzón
4 pĭŋyón	pŭŋyón	piñón	puñón
5 fĭŋhír	fŭŋhír	fingir	fungir
6 bĭ(l)yár	bŭ(l)yár	billar	bullar
7 mĭrón	mŭrón	mirón	murón
8 lĭgár	lŭgár	ligar	lugar
9 bĭrládór	bŭrládór	birlador	burlador
10 mĭsítá	mŭsítá	misita	musita
11 tĭnérŏ	tŭnérŏ	tinero	tunero
12 lĭnósŏ	lŭnósŏ	linoso	lunoso
13 mĭnítá	mŭnítá	minita	munita
14 chĭnchérŏ	chŭnchérŏ	chinchero	chunchero
15 ĭmítŏ	ŭmítŏ	imito	humito
16 mĭlítá	mŭlítá	milita	mulita
17 fĭlérŏ	fŭlérŏ	filero	fulero
18 ṣĭrkítŏ	ṣŭrkítŏ	cirquito	zurquito
19 rrĭkítá	rrŭkítá	riquita	ruquita
20 pĭḋyéndŏ	pŭḋyéndŏ	pidiendo	pudiendo

2.11.10 DRILL ON /ŏ/ VS. /ŭ/

/ŏ/	/ŭ/		
1 ŏstyón	ŭstyón	ostión	ustión

Pronunciation		Spelling	
/ŏ/	/ŭ/		
2	trŏŋkár	trŭŋkár	troncar	truncar
3	tŏpé	tŭpé	topé	tupé
4	bŏkál	bŭkál	vocal	bucal
5	ŏƀál	ŭƀál	oval	uval
6	ákŏsár	ákŭsár	acosar	acusar
7	sŏṣyêdád	sŭṣyêdád	sociedad	suciedad
8	mŏtĭlár	mŭtĭlár	motilar	mutilar
9	mŏṣĭtá	mŭsĭtá	mozita	musita
10	lŏnĭtá	lŭnĭtá	lonita	lunita
11	mŏnĭtá	mŭnĭtá	monita	munita
12	lŏnétá	lŭnétá	loneta	luneta
13	ŏmĭtŏ	ŭmĭtŏ	omito	humito
14	plŏmérŏ	plŭmérŏ	plomero	plumero
15	ŏlátê	ŭlátê	olate	ulate
16	pŏrĭtŏ	pŭrĭtŏ	porito	purito
17	sŏtáná	sŭtáná	sotana	sutana
18	sŏplĭkŏ	sŭplĭkŏ	soplico	suplico
19	rrŏkĭtá	rrŭkĭtá	roquita	ruquita
20	sŏstênĭdŏ	sŭstênĭdŏ	sostenido	sustenido

2.2 | STRONG-STRESSED VOWELS

One general observation about the English speaker's pronunciation of all simple strong-stressed vowels in Spanish except /a/ is that the English-speaker will tend to produce a diphthong instead of a monophthong. The differences between what the Spanish speaker says for these four vowels — /e/, /o/, /i/, /u/ — and what the English speaker says on first imitation, are of two types: (1) there is greater tenseness of the tongue throughout the Spanish pronunciation, and (2) the tongue and lips remain pretty much as they started, throughout the duration of the vowel, instead of changing as in English. These two differences can best be heard by direct comparison in the following lists.

2.21 ENGLISH /ey/ vs. SPANISH /e/

Instructions. — Listen to the English word and then to the Spanish word. Then repeat the Spanish words after your model, trying to avoid the influence of the similar English words.

English /ey/		Spanish /e/	
		Pronunciation	Spelling
1	day	dé	dé
2	Kay	ké	qué
3	say	sé	sé
4	bay	bé	ve
5	fay	fé	fe
6	may	mé	me
7	lay	lé	le
8	pay	pé	pe
9	hay	hé	ge
10	chay	ché	che
11	Ray	rré	re
12	way	wé	hue

Notice that the general effect of the English /ey/ is that it is longer and made up of two segments, almost as though the words were "day—ee," "Kay—ee," "say—ee," etc., whereas the Spanish words give no such effect even when they are held quite long.

2.22 ENGLISH /ow/ VS. SPANISH /o/

Instructions.—Listen to the English word and then to the Spanish word. Then repeat the Spanish words after your model, trying to avoid the influence of the similar English words.

English /ow/		Spanish /o/	
		Pronunciation	Spelling
1	know	nó	no
2	low	ló	lo
3	yoe	yó	yo
4	sew	só	so
5	Poe	pó	Po
6	tow	tó	¡to!
7	dough	dó	do
8	hoe	hó	¡jo!
9	roe	rró	ro

The effect of English /ow/, like that of /ey/, is that it is made up of two segments—"no—uu," "lo—uu," "so—uu," etc. The Spanish words do not give this effect. Note also that the lips of a Spanish speaker saying these words are rounded even as he begins the consonant before the vowel, whereas this anticipation of lip rounding occurs hardly at all in English.

2.23 ENGLISH /iy/ VS. SPANISH /i/

Instructions.—Listen to the following lists, observing how the /iy/ - /i/ difference parallels that of /ey/ - /e/. Then repeat the Spanish words after your model, trying to avoid the influence of the similar English words.

English /iy/		Spanish /i/	
		Pronunciation	Spelling
1	me	mí	mí
2	tea	tí	tí
3	see	sí	sí
4	bee	bí	vi
5	Dee	dí	di
6	knee	ní	ni

Clearly the difference is less obvious than that between /e/ and /ey/, but it is of the same type.

2.24 ENGLISH /uw/ VS. SPANISH /u/

Instructions.—Listen to the following lists, observing how the /uw/ - /u/ difference parallels the /ow/ - /o/. Then repeat the Spanish words after your model, trying to avoid the influence of the similar sounding English words.

English /uw/		Spanish /u/	
		Pronunciation	Spelling
1	two	tú	tú
2	sue	sú	su
3	pooh	pú	¡pu!
4	coo	kú	cu
5	boo	bú	bu
6	moo	mú	mu
7	foo	fú	¡fu!

It is especially noticeable in the above list that the Spanish speaker's lips are rounded when he begins the consonant but that the English speaker's are not (if he is not exaggerating his articulation).

2.3 | DIPHTHONGS

Diphthongs in Spanish are complex vowels made up of two components: (1) one of the five vowels /i/, /e/, /a/, /o/, /u/; and (2) one of the two glides, also called semivowels, /y/ and /w/. The possible diphthongs are these:

	Vy	Vw
i	-	(iw)
e	ey	ew
a	ay	aw
o	oy	(ow)
u	(uy)	-

A diphthong is always the nucleus of a single syllable. For that reason, two vowels in a sequence which are the nuclei of two successive syllables do not make up a diphthong. Thus, for example, the word "dúeto" does not contain a diphthong. If it is pronounced /dúétò/, the /u/ and /e/ belong to two different syllables. If it is pronounced /dwêtò/, there is only one vowel /e/; the u in the spelling merely represents a consonant, /w/ (to be considered as part of a cluster with the preceding /d/ giving /dw/ as in English "dwell"). There has been much confusion about diphthongs in Spanish because people have assumed that two vowel letters together represent a diphthong except when one of them is the silent u in "guerra" or "qué." The pronunciation of complex vowel sequences where more than one syllable is involved will be dealt with subsequently. The object of drill now is the true diphthong that forms the nucleus of a single syllable.

The most common Spanish diphthongs are /ey/, /ay/, /oy/, and /aw/. The same diphthongs are also quite frequent in English, but they do not sound the same as the Spanish ones. Let us examine the Spanish diphthongs by comparison with their English counterparts.

2.31 ENGLISH /ey/ VS. SPANISH /ey/

Instructions.—Listen to the English word and then to the Spanish word. Then repeat the Spanish words after your model, trying to avoid the influence of the similar English words.

English /ey/		Spanish /ey/	
		Pronunciation	Spelling
1	Ray	rréy	rey
2	lay	léy	ley
3	bay	béy	bey
4	day	déy	dey
5	base	béys	veis
6	Sayce	séys	seis
7	Dace	déys	deis
8	way	bwéy	buey

The most obvious, and most important, difference between Spanish and English in the items listed above is that the Spanish /y/ requires the tongue to glide much farther toward the front and top of the mouth than does the English /y/. Also the glide is more rapid in Spanish, and the nuclei involved are under greater tension. The following drill involves converting items which do not have the /y/ glide to items which do have it. It is important to recognize that <u>neither</u> column, /e/ or /ey/, should sound like the English /e/ of "pet" or the English /ey/ of "pate."

2.31.1 SPANISH /e/ VS. /ey/

<u>Instructions</u>.—Mimic your model's pronunciation of these items in pairs. Try to say each one of the pair exactly alike except for the minimal absence or presence of the /y/ glide. Use exactly the same intonation and stress pattern for both items of the pair. Cover the spelling.

	Pronunciation		Spelling	
	/e/	/ey/		
1	bénte	béynte	vente	veinte
2	rrénd	rréynd	reno	reino
3	bés	béys	ves	veis
4	rrés	rréys	res	reis
5	péná	péyná	pena	peina
6	pénádd	péynádd	penado	peinado
7	lé	léy	le	ley
8	rré	rréy	re	rey
9	mámé	máméy	mamé	mamey
10	káné	kánéy	cané	caney
11	yóke	yókey	lloque	yoquey

2.32 ENGLISH /ay/ VS. SPANISH /ay/

<u>Instructions</u>.—Listen to the English word and then to the Spanish word. Then repeat the Spanish words after your model, trying to avoid the influence of the similar English words.

	English /ay/	Spanish /ay/	
		Pronunciation	Spelling
1	eye	áy	hay
2	lie	láy	lay
3	"Y"	wáy	guay
4	bice	báys	vais
5	dice	dáys	dais
6	rile	rráyl	rail

Again the obviously important differences are that the Spanish /y/ glides higher and more to the front than the English /y/, the glide is faster, and the nucleus is more tense. In the following drill, the /a/ of the first column is essentially identical with the English speaker's /a/ in "pot" (not British pronunciation), but the /ay/ of the second column is different from English /ay/ in "bite."

2.32.1 SPANISH /a/ VS. /ay/

Instructions.—Mimic your model's pronunciation of these words in pairs. Try to say each one of the pair exactly alike except for the minimal absence or presence of the /y/ glide. Use exactly the same intonation and stress pattern for both members of the pair. Cover the spelling.

	Pronunciation		Spelling	
	/a/	/ay/		
1	bálà	báylà	bala	baila
2	trágò	tráygò	trago	traigo
3	árè	áyrè	are	aire
4	bánà	báynà	vana	vaina
5	gátà	gáytà	gata	gaita
6	tátà	táytà	tata	taita
7	pákò	páykò	pako	paiko
8	pàsáhè	pàysáhè	pasaje	paisaje
9	bàƀél	bàyƀél	Babel	baivel

2.33 ENGLISH /oy/ VS. SPANISH /oy/

Instructions.—Listen to the English word and then to the Spanish word. Then repeat the Spanish words after your model, trying to avoid the influence of the similar sounding English words.

English /oy/		Spanish /oy/	
		Pronunciation	Spelling
1	boy	bóy	voy
2	Doye	dóy	doy
3	soy	sóy	soy
4	oy	óy	hoy
5	coy	kóy	coy
6	Soyce	sóys	sois

From this list the same inferences can be made as those made above for /ey/ and /ay/. The glide moves higher, faster, and is tenser in Spanish.

2.33.1 SPANISH /o/ VS. /oy/

Instructions.—Mimic your model's pronunciation of these words in pairs. Try to say each one of the pair exactly alike except for the minimal absence or presence of the /y/ glide.

	Pronunciation		Spelling	
	/o/	/oy/		
1	amó	amóy	amó	Amoy
2	ó	óy	o	hoy
3	sólá	şóylá	sola	Zoila
4	kótó	kóytó	coto	coito
5	tróká	tróyká	troca	troica
6	lóká	lóyká	loca	loica
7	kómá	kóymá	coma	coima
8	bóná	bóyná	Bona	boina
9	èstóká	èstóyká	estoca	estoica

2.34 ENGLISH /aw/ VS. SPANISH /aw/

Instructions.—Listen to the English word and then to the Spanish word. Then repeat the Spanish words after your model, trying to avoid the influence of the similar English words.

	English /aw/	Spanish /aw/	
		Pronunciation	Spelling
1	how	háw	jau
2	grow(l)	gráw	Grau
3	chow	cháw	chao
4	meow	myáw	miao
5	wow	wáw	guau
6	foul	fáwl	foul
7	oun(ce)	áwn	aun
8	Taos	táws	Taos
9	owl	áwla	aula
10	howl	háwla	jaula
11	louse	láws	Laos

Two differences appear most obviously: (1) like the difference between the English and Spanish /y/ glides, the Spanish /w/ moves much farther back and the lips are more completely rounded at the end than in English, with a rapid and tense glide; (2) the first element, the vowel, begins at the /a/ position in Spanish but is farther front in many dialects of English, beginning almost with the vowel of "pat."

2.34.1 SPANISH /a/ VS. /aw/

Instructions.—Mimic your model's pronunciation of these words in pairs. Try to say each one of the pair exactly alike except for the minimal absence or presence of the /w/ glide. Try not to change the phonetic quality of the /a/ when it is followed by /w/ from the quality it has when not followed by /w/. Use exactly the same intonation and stress pattern for both members of the pair. Cover the spelling.

	Pronunciation		Spelling	
	/a/	/aw/		
1	kásâ	káwsâ	casa	causa
2	átô	áwtô	ato	auto
3	álâ	áwlâ	ala	aula
4	hálâ	háwlâ	jala	jaula
5	tás	táws	tas	Taos
6	pátâ	páwtâ	pata	pauta
7	káchô	káwchô	cacho	caucho
8	málâ	máwlâ	mala	maula
9	fánô	fáwnô	fano	fauno
10	gáchô	gáwchô	gacho	gaucho
11	êmbâlár	êmbâwlár	embalar	embaular

2.35 OTHER DIPHTHONGS

The other diphthongs are relatively rare and cause little difficulty for that reason. /uy/ alternates freely with /wi/—that is, a word like "cuidado" may be pronounced wither [kûyđáđô] or [kwiđáđô]. /iw/ alternates freely with /yu/—that is, a word like "ciudad" may be pronounced either [şiwđáđ] or [şyûđáđ]. /ow/ occurs only in personal names and a very few other items. /ew/ is worth a short drill.

2.35.1 SPANISH /e/ VS. /ew/

Instructions.—Mimic your model's pronunciation of these words in pairs. Try to say each member of the pair exactly alike except for the minimal absence or presence of the /w/ glide.

	Pronunciation		Spelling	
	/e/	/ew/		
1	déđô	déwđô	dedo	deudo
2	rrémâ	rréwmâ	rema	reuma
3	léđô	léwđô	ledo	leudo
4	némâ	néwmâ	nema	neuma
5	têtón	têwtón	tetón	Teutón

2.4 | VARIETIES OF /e/ IN SPANISH

The four vowels /i/, /a/, /o/, and /u/ are remarkably stable and unvaried in their phonetic quality. They do not show much change in relation to the other sounds with which they appear in words. But /e/ is quite a different matter, at least from the point of view of English speakers.

When /e/ is at the end of a Spanish syllable, it is generally a phonetically higher vowel—like the vowel of English "mate" but without diphthongization—than when it is followed by a consonant in the same syllable. When it is followed by a consonant in the same syllable (and some consonants have this effect much more than others), it tends to be a phonetically lower vowel—more like the vowel of English "met." The variation is always non-significant, but it is worth the trouble of learning to imitate it accurately and to put the right variety of /e/ in the right environment. Not all Spanish speakers distribute the varieties in exactly the same way, and you should not be at all disturbed to find such discrepancy existing on this level, where the difference is not significant—i.e., does not correlate with differences in meanings.

2.41 VARIETIES OF /e/

Instructions.—Mimic your model's pronunciation of these items in pairs. Observe whether he makes a difference in the quality of the vowel or not and imitate whatever he does.

	Pronunciation		Spelling	
	Higher variety [e]	Lower variety [ɛ]		
1	méså	méstå	mesa	mesta
2	séså	séstå	cesa	cesta
3	péså	péskå	pesa	pesca
4	sésò	séstò	seso	sexto
5	sélå	séltå	cela	celta
6	sélå	séldå	cela	celda
7	bénå	béntå	vena	venta
8	bénå	béŋgå	vena	venga
9	ténå	téŋgå	tena	tenga
10	syénå	syéntå	siena	sienta
11	pérå	pérlå	pera	perla
12	òtélò	òtél	Otelo	hotel
13	påpé	påpél	papé	papel
14	dé	dél	de	del
15	nìbé	nìbél	ni ve	nivel
16	påsté	påstél	pasté	pastel
17	plånté	plåntél	planté	plantel

	Pronunciation		Spelling	
	Higher variety [e]	Lower variety [ɛ]		
18	tòné	tònél	toné	tonel
19	kómè	kómên	come	comen
20	bíbè	bíbên	vive	viven

2.5 | MISCELLANEOUS ENGLISH INFLUENCE

There are many words in Spanish which sound rather similar to familiar English words. When a student hears one of these Spanish words, his mimicry of them flows smoothly into the familiar English channels. He will make certain mistakes in the vowels of the Spanish word which he probably would not make in a word with no familiar ring. Typical lists of these words follow; they should give the student no difficulty after he becomes aware of the kind of error English is leading him into.

2.51 SPANISH /o/ VS. ENGLISH /ɑ/

Instructions.—Mimic your model's pronunciation of the Spanish items in Column A, comparing the correct pronunciation with the common erroneous one shown in Column B, and comparing this error with the quite normal English pronunciation shown phonetically in Column C. You will very probably need guidance from your instructor in interpreting the phonetic symbols for English, but your own normal pronunciation will illustrate the differences.

Spanish			English	
Spelling	Correct pronunciation A	Probable error B	Pronunciation C	Spelling
oficina	òfìsínà	àfìsínà	áfɨs	office
doctor	dòktór	dàktór	dáktɨr	doctor
congreso	kòngrésò	kàngrésò	káŋgrɨs	congress
conferencia	kòmfèrénsyá	kàmfèrénsyá	kánfɨrɨnts	conference
Honduras	òndúràs	àndúràs	hàndúrɨs	Honduras
posible	pòsíblé	pàsíblé	pásɨbɨl	possible
loteria	lòtèría	làtèría	látɨriy	lottery
producto	pròdúktò	pràdúktò	prádəkt	product
oportunidad	òpòrtùnidád	àpòrtùnidád	àpɨrtúwnɨtiy	opportunity
contrario	kòntráryò	kàntráryò	kántrɛriy	contrary
tropical	tròpíkál	tràpíkál	trápɨkɨl	tropical
chocolate	chòkòláté	chàkòláté	chákɨlɨt	chocolate
operador	òpèràdór	àpèràdór	ápɨrèytɨr	operator

Spanish			English	
Spelling	Correct pronunciation A	Probable error B	Pronunciation C	Spelling
conversación	kọmbẹrsás̨yón	kạ́mbẹrsás̨yón	kạ̀nvɨrséyšɨn	conversation
responsabilidad	rrẹspọ̀nsabilidad	rrẹspạ̀nsabilidád	rɨspạ̀nsɨbílɨtly	responsibility
hospital	ọspitál	ạ̲spitál	hạ́spɨtɨl	hospital
contrato	kọntráto	kạ́ntráto	kạ́ntrækt	contract
bombardeo	bọ̀mbárdéó	bạ̀mbárdéó	bạ̀mbárd	bombard
operación	ọ̀pẹ̀rás̨yón	ạ̲̀pẹ̀rás̨yón	ạ̀pɨréyšɨn	operation
pronto	prọ́ntò	prạ́ntò	prạ́ntòw	pronto
próxima	prọ́ksimá	prạ́ksimá	ɨprạ́ksɨmɨt	approximate
fósforo	fọ́sfọ̀ró	fạ́sfọ̀ró	fạ́sfɨrɨs	phosphorous
costo	kọ́stò	kạ́stò	kạ́st	cost
bomba	bọ́mbá	bạ́mbá	bạ́m	bomb
dólares	dọ́lárès	dạ́lárès	dạ́lɨrz	dollars

2.52 SPANISH /a/ VS. ENGLISH /æ/

Instructions.—Mimic your model's pronunciation of the Spanish items in Column A, comparing the correct pronunciation with the common erroneous one shown in Column B, and comparing this error with the quite normal English pronunciation shown phonetically in Column C. You will very probably need guidance from your instructor in interpreting the phonetic symbols for English, but your own normal pronunciation will illustrate the differences.

Spanish			English	
Spelling	Correct pronunciation A	Probable error B	Pronunciation C	Spelling
blanca	blạ́ŋkạ̀	blǽŋkạ̀	blǽŋk	blank
Kansas	kánsạ̀s	kǽnsạ̀s	kǽnzɨz	Kansas
pase	pásè	pǽsè	pǽs	pass
clase	klásè	klǽsè	klǽs	class
gracias	grás̨yạ̀s	grǽs̨yạ̀s	grǽs	grass
lástima	lástimạ̀	lǽstimạ̀	lǽst	last
español	èspạ̀ŋyól	èspǽŋyól	spǽnɨš	Spanish
absoluto	ạ̀bsòlútò	ǽbsòlútò	ǽbsɨlùwt	absolute
campo	kámpò	kǽmpò	kǽmp	camp
saco	sákò	sǽkò	sǽk	sack
fábrica	fábrɨkạ̀	fǽbrɨkạ̀	fǽbrɨk	fabric
francamente	frạ̀ŋkạ̀méntè	fræ̀ŋkạ̀méntè	frǽŋklly	frankly
grande	grạ́ndè	grǽndè	grǽnd	grand

Spanish			English	
Spelling	Correct pronunciation A	Probable error B	Pronunciation C	Spelling
mecánico	mèkánìkò	mèkǽnìkò	mɪkǽnɪk	mechanic
taxi	táksɪ	tǽksɪ	tǽksɪy	taxi
aniversario	ànìbèrsáryò	ænìbèrsáryò	æ̀nɪvɪrsɪry	anniversary
aspirina	àspɪrínà	æspɪrínà	æspɪrɪn	aspirin

Before the next such list of words is presented for drill, a brief explanation is needed of the symbols to be used. The symbol /i/ is used in transcribing Spanish to represent a vowel very much like the English vowel in "beet" /bíyt/, though tenser and without the glide shown by the /y/. The same symbol /i/ is used in transcribing English to symbolize the vowel of "bit" /bít/; that is, "beet" is different from "bit" by virtue of the /y/ glide and the additional tenseness supplied by that glide. The use of the symbol /i/ both for the vowel of English "bit" and Spanish "sí" may easily be confusing. For this reason, in the following list the phonetic transcription of English will show the vowel of "bit" with the symbol [ɪ] instead of [i] merely to remind the reader that it is a different sound from the vowel of "sí."

2.53 SPANISH /i/ VS. ENGLISH [ɪ]

Instructions.—Mimic your model's pronunciation of the Spanish items in Column A, comparing the correct pronunciation with the common erroneous one shown in Column B, and comparing this error with the quite normal English pronunciation shown phonetically in Column C.

Spanish			English	
Spelling	Correct pronunciation A	Probable error B	Pronunciation C	Spelling
diplomático	dìplòmátìkò	dɪplòmátɪkò	dɪ̀plɪmǽtɪk	diplomatic
magnificas	màgnifíkàs	màgnɪfíkàs	mægnɪfɪsɪnt	magnificent
fábrica	fábrìkà	fábrɪkà	fǽbrɪk	fabric
décima	déṣìmà	déṣɪmà	désɪmɪl	decimal
México	méhìkò	méhɪkò	méksɪkòw	Mexico
oficina	òfìṣínà	òfɪṣínà	áfɪs	office
interés	ìntèrés	ìntɪrés	ɪ́ntɪrɪst	interest
interesante	ìntèrèsántè	ìntɪrɪsántè	ɪ́ntrɪstɪŋ	interesting
Italia	ìtályà	ɪtályà	ɪ́tɪly	Italy
inteligente	ìntèlìhéntè	ɪntɪlɪhéntè	ɪntélɪʤɪnt	intelligent
interior	ìntèryór	ɪntɪryór	ɪntíryɪr	interior

Spanish			English	
Spelling	Correct pronunciation A	Probable error B	Pronunciation C	Spelling
informacion	ımfȯrmȧ̧sўón	ımfȯrmȧ̧sўón	ìnfɨrméyšɨn	information
imposible	ımpȯsíblė	ımpȯsíblė	ımpásɨbɨl	impossible
invitar	ımbıtár	ımbıtár	ınváyt	invite
dinero	dınérȯ	dınérȯ	dínɨr	dinner
divorsiado	dıbȯrsўádȯ	dıbȯrsўádȯ	dıvȯ́rst	divorced
distancia	dıstáṇsўȧ	dıstáṇsўȧ	dístɨnts	distance
disgusto	dızgústȯ	dızgústȯ	dısgɨ́st	disgust
minuto	mınútȯ	mınútȯ	mínɨt	minute
Nicaragua	nıkȧrágwȧ	nıkȧrágwȧ	nìkɨrágwɨ	Nicaragua
firmar	fırmár	fırmár	fír	fear
sistema	sıstémȧ	sıstémȧ	sístɨm	system
solicito	sȯlı̧sítȯ	sȯlı̧sítȯ	sɨlísɨt	solicit

<table>
<tr><td>2.6</td><td>CONTIGUOUS VOWEL SEQUENCES</td></tr>
</table>

Spanish is a language in which a great many words end with vowels, and a great many begin with vowels. It therefore often happens that two vowels occur in adjacent syllables. Then various kinds of modifications of one or the other or both vowels take place, depending on what vowels are involved.

As a general rule the same vowel does not repeat itself from one word to the next in Spanish. What would be two identical adjacent vowels in slow speed appear in normal speed simply as one single vowel.

2.61 MODIFICATION OF ADJACENT IDENTICAL VOWELS

Instructions.—Mimic your model's pronunciation of the items in Columns B and C, bearing in mind that only Column C is appropriate at normal speed. The symbol /˘/ placed over a vowel means that the vowel is syllabic but very short and fast.

Pronunciation			Spelling
Components A	Slow speed B	Normal speed C	
/ii/			
mi—íhȯ	mĭíhȯ	míhȯ	mi hijo
si—ilústrȧ	sĭilústrȧ	sılústrȧ	si ilustra
ni—ınés	nĭınés	ninés	ni Inés

	Pronunciation		Spelling
Components A	Slow speed B	Normal speed C	
/ee/			
dĕ—éstá	dĕĕstá	déstá	de esta
ké—ĕstá	kéĕstá	késtá	¿qué está?
sĕ—échá	sĕĕcha	sécha	se echa
/aa/			
bá—à—komér	báăkòmér	bákòmér	va a comer
ĕstá—àşyéndò	ĕstáăşyéndò	ĕstáşyéndò	está haciendo
là—ámà	lăámà	lámà	la ama
/oo/			
lò—ótrò	lŏŏtrò	lótrò	lo otro
óchò—ómbrês	óchŏŏmbrês	óchómbrês	ocho hombres
nó—óy̆ês	nŏóy̆ês	nóy̆ês	¿no oyes?
/uu/			
sù—últimò	sŭúltimò	súltimò	su último
tù—úmò	tŭúmò	túmò	tu humo
sù—ùnifórmê	sŭŭnifórmê	sùnifórmê	su uniforme

When there are two different vowels occurring contiguously in adjacent sylla-bles, the pattern of modification is somewhat more complex. When the first of the vowels is /i/ or /u/, it may change to /y/ or /w/.

2.62 MODIFICATION OF ADJACENT VOWELS, /iV/ OR /uV/

Instructions.—Mimic your model's pronunciation of the items in Columns B and C, noting especially the difference in syllabicity of /i/ and /u/ by com-parison with /y/ and /w/.

	Pronunciation		Spelling
Components A	Slow speed B	Normal speed C	
/ie/ mĭ—ĕstílò	mĭĕstílò	my̆ĕstílò	mi estilo
/ia/ mĭ—áchà	mĭáchà	my̆áchà	mi hacha
/io/ mĭ—ótrò	mĭótrò	my̆ótrò	mi otro
/iu/ mĭ—úņyà	mĭúņyà	my̆úņyà	mi uña
/ui/ sù—íhà	sŭíhà	swíhà	su hija
/ue/ sù—ĕstílò	sŭĕstílò	swĕstílò	su estilo
/ua/ sù—áchà	sŭáchà	swáchà	su hacha
/uo/ sù—ótrò	sŭótrò	swótrò	su otro

When the first of the two vowels is /e/ or /o/, three possibilities exist: full syllabic length (marked by the dot over the vowel below), short syllabic length (marked by the breve over the vowel), or reduction to semivowel or zero. When the first vowel is /a/, the same possibilities exist except that the final reduction must be to zero, not to semivowel.

2.63 MODIFICATION OF ADJACENT VOWELS, /eV/, /oV/, /aV/

Instructions.—Mimic your model's pronunciation of the items in Columns B, C, and D, noting the differences in length and syllabicity.

		Pronunciation		Spelling
Components A	Slow speed B	Normal speed C	Fast normal D	
/ei/ dè—íntǐmŏ	dĕíntǐmŏ	dĕíntǐmŏ	díntǐmŏ	de íntimo
/ea/ dè—áchǎ	dĕáchǎ	dĕáchǎ	dyáchǎ	de hacha
/eo/ dè—ótrŏ	dĕótrŏ	dĕótrŏ	dyótrŏ	de otro
/eu/ dè—útǐl	dĕútǐl	dĕútǐl	dyútǐl	de útil
/oi/ lŏ—íntǐmŏ	lŏíntǐmŏ	lŏíntǐmŏ	lwíntǐmŏ	lo íntimo
/oe/ lŏ—échŏ	lŏéchŏ	lŏéchŏ	lwéchŏ	lo hecho
/oa/ lŏ—ábǐl	lŏábǐl	lŏábǐl	lwábǐl	lo hábil
/ou/ lŏ—útǐl	lŏútǐl	lŏútǐl	lútǐl	lo útil
/ai/ lǎ—íhǎ	lǎíhǎ	lǎíhǎ	líhǎ	la hija
/ae/ lǎ—émbrǎ	lǎémbrǎ	lǎémbrǎ	lémbrǎ	la hembra
/ao/ lǎ—ótrǎ	lǎótrǎ	lǎótrǎ	lótrǎ	la otra
/au/ lǎ—úŋyǎ	lǎúŋyǎ	lǎúŋyǎ	lúŋyǎ	la uña

2.7 | SUMMING-UP OF VOWELS

One has but to listen to three English speakers say the word "house"—one from Richmond, Virginia, one from Cleveland, Ohio, and the third from Austin, Texas—to know that the occurrence of vowels in English varies from one part of the country to another. A person with sufficient knowledge and practice can use the vowels of a speaker's dialect to fix rather exactly his area of origin.

Spanish speakers, on the other hand, do not readily reveal their area of origin through the vowels they use. The vowel system is remarkably stable and unvarying throughout the Spanish speaking world. All over, the facts are pretty much as they have been described in these pages. But the consonants are more varied by far, and geographical origins are easily perceived through consonant variations. Our discussion and drill will therefore have to be somewhat normalized, and observations about dialect differences will have to be made from time to time.

THE CONSONANTS | 3

Consonants are different from vowels in that they are never the center of syllables. Consonants always involve some kind of restriction in the free flow of air through the mouth. The articulation of each consonant will be discussed in detail in its own turn. The discussion below is intended only to familiarize you with some rather general facts about the articulation of consonants.

As the air is pushed up from the lungs, it may be stopped completely by closing the lips or by pushing the tongue up against some part of the roof of the mouth; if it is then released abruptly, the effect is to produce a consonant that is known as a stop. English words like "pill, till, kill, bill, dill, gill" all begin with stop consonants.

Instead of stopping the air completely, it is possible to restrict its flow tightly by narrowing the passage at some point. The result will be that friction is created at that point, just as the narrowing of a river produces rapids. Sounds produced in this way are known as spirants or fricatives. English words like "fill, sill, shell, veal, zeal" all begin with spirant consonants.

Stop and spirant articulations can be combined to produce what are known as affricates. "Chill" and "Jill" are English words that begin with affricates.

While stopping the air in the mouth, it is possible to let the air continue flowing freely through the nose. Consonants made in this way are called nasal continuants. "Mile" and "Nile" are English words which begin with nasal continuants.

The tip of the tongue can be raised in such a way that the air is forced to flow around one side of it, or both sides. A consonant made in this way is called a lateral continuant. English words like "Lil" and "less" begin with this consonant.

While any consonant is being articulated, the vocal cords may be vibrating or they may be held apart so that they are not vibrating. If they are vibrating, the resultant sound is said to be voiced. If not, it is voiceless. Voiced consonants in English include the first sounds of "bill, dill, gill" (voiced stops), or "veal" and "zeal" (voiced spirants), of "Jill" (voiced affricate), and of "mill, nil, Lil" (voiced nasal and lateral continuants). Voiceless consonants include the first sounds of "pill, till, kill" (voiceless stops), of "fill, sill, shell" (voiceless spirants), and of "chill" (voiceless affricate). One way to determine whether a sound is voiced or not is to place your fingers over your throat while saying the sound; if there is vibration, it is voiced. In making this test, be sure you do not say a vowel along with the consonant, since all vowels are voiced.

3.1 | THE VOICED STOP-SPIRANTS

The most important of the voiced stop-spirants is /d/. It is similar sometimes to one English sound, the /d/ of "den," and at other times to quite a different English sound, the /ð/ of "then." /d/ is a voiced stop; /ð/ is a voiced spirant. The Spanish
stop is articulated like the English /d/, but with the tip of the tongue touching the back side
of the upper teeth, whereas it touches somewhat farther back in English. The Spanish /d/
is therefore <u>dental</u> in articulation, whereas the English is <u>alveolar</u>—that is, in English the
tongue touches the rough ridge behind the upper teeth, the alveolar ridge. The Spanish spirant, indicated in the respelling with a small line through the bowl of the <u>d</u>, is much like
the first sound of English words like "these, that, then, there," or the middle sound of "either, mother, father, brother, dither"; but it is a good deal more relaxed in articulation.
A close approximation to the Spanish sound [ð] can be made by pronouncing words like
"mother, father," etc., as an inebriated person might be expected to, softening the medial
English <u>th</u>.

In the exercise below, all the words in the first column have a stop [d], in the
second column a spirant [ð].

3.11 SPANISH [d] VS. [ð]

<u>Instructions</u>.—Mimic your model's pronunciation of the following items in
pairs. Notice the positions where a [d] appears as compared with where a
[ð] appears.

	Pronunciation		Spelling	
	[d]	[ð]		
1	dá	áðá	da	hada
2	dí	íðá	di	ida
3	dán	náðá	dan	nada
4	dómá	móðá	doma	moda
5	dó	óðá	do	oda
6	dótó	tóðó	doto	todo
7	dúná	núðá	duna	nuda
8	dóló	lóðó	dolo	lodo
9	dáká	káðá	daca	cada
10	séndá	séðá	senda	seda
11	óndá	óðá	honda	oda
12	dándó	dáðó	dando	dado
13	ándá	áðá	anda	hada
14	móndó	móðó	mondo	modo
15	bándó	báðó	bando	bado
16	gíndó	gíðó	guindo	guido
17	múndó	múðó	mundo	mudo

Pronunciation		Spelling	
[d]	[đ]		
18 yéndŏ	yéđŏ	yendo	hiedo
19 fyándŏ	fyáđŏ	fiando	fiado
20 pŏndré	pŏđré	pondré	podré
21 şéldă	şéđă	celda	ceda
22 báldĕ	báđĕ	balde	vade
23 móldă	móđă	molda	moda
24 káldă	káđă	calda	cada
25 áldă	áđă	halda	hada
26 fáldă	fáđă	falda	fada
27 áldábă	áđábă	aldaba	adaba

From the examples it appears that [d] is the sound which can occur at the beginning of utterance, and after /n/ or /l/. Otherwise the variety of the sound must be the spirant. A single word like "dedo" or "dado" or "adónde" will have both varieties in it: [déđŏ], [dáđŏ], and [ađóndĕ]. Clearly, in English, [d] and [đ] are in contrast, as illustrated by "den" vs. "then," "fodder" vs. "father," "laid" vs. "lathe," and so on. But, in Spanish, [d] and [đ] are never in contrast. Rather, they supplement each other, one of them occurring where the other cannot. You must learn to use each automatically in its proper place.

There are still other problems associated with the Spanish /d/. One is the fact that if you use an ordinary English /d/ in certain situations, it will sound like an /r/ to a Spanish speaker. In the exercise below, every word in the left-hand column that you pronounce with a Spanish [d] instead of a Spanish [đ] will be misheard as having been pronounced with a Spanish [r]. On the other hand, the words in the right-hand column can be pronounced with an ordinary English /d/ and, if spoken rapidly, they will pass as having a Spanish [r].

3.11.1 SPANISH /d/ IN ITS [đ] VARIANT VS. SPANISH /r/

Instructions.—Mimic your model's pronunciation of the following items in pairs, being sure you distinguish between them in the same way he does.

Pronunciation		Spelling	
[đ]	[r]		
1 áđă	áră	hada	ara
2 óđă	óră	oda	hora
3 píđă	píră	pida	pira
4 púđŏ	púrŏ	pudo	puro
5 báđŏ	bárŏ	vado	varo
6 béđă	béră	veda	vera

Pronunciation		Spelling	
[đ]	[r]		
7	tóđò	tórò	todo	toro
8	dúđò	dúrò	dudo	duro
9	káđà	kárà	cada	cara
10	kóđò	kórò	codo	coro
11	míđò	mírò	mido	miro
12	múđò	múrò	mudo	muro
13	móđò	mórò	modo	moro
14	séđà	sérà	seda	sera
15	háđà	hárà	jada	jara
16	húđàs	húràs	Judas	juras
17	lóđò	lórò	lodo	loro
18	ɏóđò	ɏórò	yodo	lloro

Another problem of the /d/ comes from the way in which English speakers pronounce words like "bidden," "hidden," and "gladden." They say what sounds like "bid'n," "hid'n," "gladd'n." Phoneticians often transcribe such words as [bíd̩n], [híd̩n], [glǽd̩n]. When English speakers come to Spanish words like "piden" or "pidan," which are very common, they tend to carry over the same habit.

3.11.2 SPANISH /d/ before /Vn/

Instructions.—Mimic your model's pronunciation of the following items in pairs, being careful to make the last vowel of the two-syllable words sound like the vowel of the one-syllable words.

Pronunciation		Spelling	
[dV́n]	[᷄đVn]		
1	dán	kéđán	dan	quedan
2	dén	kéđén	den	queden
3	dán	míđán	dan	midan
4	dén	míđén	den	miden
5	dán	píđán	dan	pidan
6	dén	píđén	den	piden
7	dán	béđán	dan	vedan
8	dén	béđén	den	veden
9	dán	náđán	dan	nadan
10	dén	náđén	den	naden
11	dán	șéđán	dan	cedan
12	dén	șéđén	den	ceden
13	dán	gwárđán	dan	guardan

	Pronunciation		Spelling	
	[dV́n]	[-́đVn]		
14	dén	gwárđên	den	guarden
15	dán	gráđân	dan	gradan
16	dén	gráđên	den	graden
17	dán	trâzláđân	dan	trasladan
18	dén	trâzláđên	den	trasladen

The second of the Spanish voiced stop-spirants is /b/, with two variants that are transcribed [b] and [ƀ]. The [b] is in most respects identical with English /b/ and causes no difficulty. [ƀ], on the other hand, is a sound which does not exist in English. It partly resembles the English /v/, but [v] is a sound which does not exist in Spanish except in hyperurban "spelling" pronunciations. The fact that it exists in the spelling, though not in normal pronunciation, has resulted in these hyperurbanisms.

There are two differences between English /v/ and Spanish [ƀ]. English /v/ is a spirant produced by pressing the lower lip back toward the upper teeth. Spanish [ƀ] is a spirant produced by pressing the lower lip up toward the upper lip. In neither case is the air stopped. A second difference is the more relaxed articulation of Spanish [ƀ]. If the English b sound in words like "rubber, Hubbel, hubby, Moby" is produced in a very relaxed way, much as an inebriated person might be expected to, the result will be fairly close to Spanish [ƀ].

3.12 SPANISH [b] VS. [ƀ]

Instructions.—Mimic your model's pronunciation of the following items in pairs. Notice the conditions under which a [b] appears as against those under which a [ƀ] appears, and compare them with the conditions for [d] and [đ]. Notice also that the spelling of b or v has nothing to do with which variety of /b/ occurs in speech.

	Pronunciation		Spelling	
	[b]	[ƀ]		
1	bá	áƀâ	va	haba
2	bé	éƀâ	ve	Eva
3	bí	íƀâ	vi	iba
4	bú	úƀâ	bu	uva
5	bótâ	tóƀâ	bota	toba
6	bólâ	lóƀâ	bola	loba
7	bárrô	rráƀô	barro	rabo
8	bórrâ	rróƀâ	borra	roba
9	bákâ	káƀâ	vaca	cava
10	bánô	náƀô	vano	nabo

Pronunciation		Spelling	
[b]	[ƀ]		
11 bákė	kábė	vaque	cabe
12 ámbàs	áƀàs	ambas	habas
13 támbò	táƀò	tambo	tabo
14 bémbò	béƀò	bembo	bebo
15 ʂúmbà	súƀà	zumba	suba
16 émbrà	éƀrà	hembra	hebra
17 túmbà	túƀà	tumba	tuba
18 ómbrė	óƀrė	hombre	obre
19 ámbrė	áƀrė	hambre	abre
20 kúmbrė	kúƀrė	cumbre	cubre

From the examples it appears that [b] is the sound which can occur at the beginning of utterance, and after /m/. Otherwise the variety of the sound must be [ƀ], even after /l/, as in [álƀà] "alba," and [pólƀò] "polvo." The distribution of the two varieties of /b/ is therefore similar to that of /d/, but not quite the same. Both varieties of /b/ can be heard in single words like [beƀér] "beber," [biƀír] "vivir," [bíƀė] "vive," and many others.

The last of the Spanish stop-spirants is /g/. Like /b/, its stop variety [g] occurs only at the beginning and after a nasal, in this case /n/ rather than /m/. The spirant variety [g] is a sound which does not exist in English, but an English speaker can rather easily learn to produce it by holding his tongue down with a finger while he attempts to say "ago." Since his finger prevents the tongue from making contact with the back part of the roof of the mouth, the only possible result is the spirant [g]. Both varieties of /g/ can be heard in a word like [gágá] "gaga." Another device to help produce the sound [g] is to pronounce English words like "sugar, foggy, baggy, beggar," in a very relaxed way, much as an inebriated person might be expected to. Softening the syllable-dividing English g will result in a sound very close to Spanish [g].

3.13 SPANISH [g] VS. [g]

Instructions.—Mimic your model's pronunciation of the following items in pairs.

Pronunciation		Spelling	
[g]	[g]		
1 gótà	tógà	gota	toga
2 gásà	ságà	gasa	saga
3 gósà	sógà	gosa	soga
4 gá(l)ɏà	(l)ɏágà	galla	llaga
5 gálò	lágò	galo	lago

Pronunciation		Spelling	
[g]	[g̶]		
6 gódð	dógð	godo	dogo
7 máŋgð	mágð	mango	mago
8 gáŋgá	gágá	ganga	gaga
9 àŋgóstð	àgóstð	angosto	agosto
10 sàŋgrádð	sàgrádð	sangrado	sagrado
11 lwéŋgð	lwégð	luengo	luego

3.2 | VIBRANTS AND LATERALS

The Spanish consonant that probably gives the most trouble to English speakers is /r/. To master it, you must practice it in quite a number of different situations. The place to begin is with the one you were introduced to in exercise 3.11.1, the one which so closely resembles the English /d/ in words like "shudder, rudder, ladder, lady, muddy, heady," and so on. It is called a flap, or a one-tap trill. In British English, it passes for /r/ in some styles of saying words like "very (veddy), merry (meddy), courage (cottage)." It is made by tensing the tongue along the bottom of the mouth and then springing it up against the roof of the mouth and right back down again, much as a piece of thin metal springs back into place after being slightly bent.

It is not difficult to produce the /r/ when it is between two syllables the first of which is stressed more strongly than the second. Simply carry over the habit of flapping the English /d/ in the same way. But when the stress is on the second of the two syllables, there is no English habit to carry over, since /d/ at the beginning of a stressed syllable in English is quite different from the Spanish /r/.

3.21 SPANISH /ˊr-/ VS. /-rˊ/

Instructions.—Mimic your model's pronunciation of the following items in pairs. Under no conditions should you substitute an ordinary American r sound. The /r/ in both columns should sound the same.

Pronunciation		Spelling	
/ˊr-/	/-rˊ/		
1 árð	àró	aro	aró
2 írà	ìrá	ira	irá
3 párð	pàró	paro	paró
4 bírð	bìró	viro	viró
5 bárð	bàró	varo	varó
6 mírð	mìró	miro	miró
7 (l)yórð	(l)yòró	lloro	lloró

Pronunciation		Spelling	
/ˊr-/	/-rˊ/		
8 húrð	húró	juro	juró
9 báryð	báryó	bario	varió
10 áspírð	áspíró	aspiro	aspiró
11 éspérð	éspéró	espero	esperó
12 ópérð	ópéró	opero	operó
13 órá	órál	hora	oral
14 kórá	kórán	Cora	Korán
15 kárá	káráy	cara	caray
16 tórá	tórál	tora	toral
17 mórá	mórál	mora	moral
18 pérð	pérón	pero	Perón
19 flórá	flórál	flora	floral
20 pírá	pírál	pira	piral
21 kárá	kárákás	cara	Caracas
22 párá	párádá	para	parada
23 árá	árádð	ara	arado
24 kóró	kórónä	coro	corona
25 pírá	pírátá	pira	pirata

Because of the similarity between the Spanish /r/ in certain positions and the English /d/ in certain positions, the following drill is needed to clarify the differences that exist in Spanish itself between /r/, /d/, and /rd/.

3.21.1 SPANISH [ˊr-], [ˊd-], AND [ˊrd-]

Instructions.—Mimic your model's pronunciation of the following series of three items.

Pronunciation			Spelling		
[ˊr-]	[ˊd-]	[ˊrd-]			
1 órá	óðá	órðá	hora	oda	orda
2 árá	áðá	árðá	ara	hada	arda
3 kárá	káðá	kárðá	cara	cada	carda
4 tórð	tóðð	tórðð	toro	todo	tordo
5 kórá	kóðá	kórðá	Cora	coda	corda
6 bárð	báðð	bárðð	varo	vado	bardo
7 şérá	şéðá	şérðá	cera	ceda	cerda
8 şérð	şéðð	şérðð	cero	cedo	cerdo

The problem that everyone anticipates with Spanish /r/ is the production of /rr/, the full trill. This sound is found in some dialects of English (often among telephone

operators) when they say, with great emphasis, "thu—rrreee" for "three." For most people, it is a completely new sound and difficult to learn to produce. There is no description
that will help you produce it. Only imitation of your instructor will do it.

3.21.2 SPANISH /r/ VS. /rr/

Instructions.—Mimic your model's pronunciation of the following items in
pairs. Do not substitute an American /r/ sound for either one of the pair.

	Pronunciation		Spelling	
	/r/	/rr/		
1	péro	pérro	pero	perro
2	káro	kárro	caro	carro
3	párá	párrá	para	parra
4	bárá	bárrá	vara	barra
5	kóro	kórro	coro	corro
6	ṣéro	ṣérro	cero	cerro
7	yéro	yérro	hiero	hierro
8	fóro	fórro	foro	forro
9	fyéro	fyérro	fiero	fierro
10	ámárá	ámárrá	amara	amarra

The /rr/ occurs not only between vowels but also at the beginning of words.
Of course, if the preceding word ends in a vowel, then the occurrence at the beginning of
the word is the same as between vowels. But at the very beginning of an utterance, the
/rr/ often occurs and sounds slightly different from its sound between vowels.

3.21.3 SPANISH /rr/ INITIALLY

Instructions.—Mimic your model's pronunciation of the following items in
pairs.

	Pronunciation		Spelling	
	/rr-/	/-rr-/		
1	rrábo	bárro	rabo	barro
2	rráchá	chárrá	racha	charra
3	rráfá	fárrá	rafa	farra
4	rráhá	hárrá	raja	jarra
5	rrápá	párrá	rapa	parra
6	rrákétá	kárrétá	raqueta	carreta
7	rrátó	tárro	rato	tarro
8	rreṣétá	ṣérrétá	receta	cerreta
9	rráná	nárrá	rana	narra

Pronunciation		Spelling	
/rr-/	/-rr-/		
10 rróká	kórrá	roca	corra
11 rrópá	pórrá	ropa	porra
12 rrútá	túrrá	ruta	turra
13 rróṣó	ṣórró	rozo	zorro
14 rróbá	bórrá	roba	borra

Spanish /r/ is as obviously different from English /r/ when adjacent to a consonant as it is in the positions already examined. After a consonant, it is a single flap of the tongue, much like the single /r/ between vowels. If you have trouble with it, you may find it helpful to say /pr-/ as though it were [pd-], /tr/ as though it were [td-], and so on. The [-d-] must be very quick, however, and there can be no vowel between it and the preceding consonant. Before a consonant, the /r/ may be a single flap or a full trill, depending on the degree of emphasis, style of speech, and so on.

3.21.4 SPANISH /Cr-/ AND /-rC/

Instructions.—Mimic your model's pronunciation of the following items in pairs.

Pronunciation		Spelling	
/Cr-/	/-rC/		
1 présá	sérpá	presa	serpa
2 tráká	kártá	traca	carta
3 krétá	térká	creta	terca
4 brágá	gárbá	braga	garba
5 drógá	górdá	droga	gorda
6 grábá	bárgá	graba	varga
7 frágá	gárfá	fraga	garfa

There are, of course, many other consonants that combine with /r/ besides the ones included above, but if the ones above are produced easily, the others will give no trouble. For additional practice if it is needed, some of them are listed below.

3.21.5 SPANISH /Cr-/ AND /-rC/, MISCELLANEOUS

Instructions.—Mimic your model's pronunciation of the following items in rows.

Pronunciation		Spelling	
/Cr-/	/-rC/		
1 próntó	kwérpó	pronto	cuerpo
2 prímó	tórpè	primo	torpe

Pronunciation		Spelling	
/Cr-/	/-rC/		
3	trés	kártâ	tres	carta
4	trátô	pwértâ	trato	puerta
5	krúdô	şérkâ	crudo	cerca
6	kréô	párkê	creo	parque
7	brâsíl	árbôl	Brasil	árbol
8	brómâ	kúrьâ	broma	curva
9	drámâ	tárdê	drama	tarde
10	drógâ	gwárdâ	droga	guarda
11	grásyâs	gárgántâ	gracias	garganta
12	grándê	âmárgô	grande	amargo
13	fríô	mârfíl	frío	marfil
14	frásê	pêrfíl	frase	perfil
15	. . .	fársâ	. . .	farsa
16	. . .	írsê	. . .	irse
17	. . .	ârhêntínâ	. . .	Argentina
18	. . .	sûrhyó	. . .	surgió
19	. . .	dôrmí	. . .	dormí
20	. . .	ármâ	. . .	arma
21	. . .	byérnês	. . .	viernes
22	. . .	órnô	. . .	horno

Spanish /r/ is likely to be especially difficult for English speakers when it occurs twice within two adjacent syllables. The most common situation in which this occurs is when one /r/ is between vowels and the other is after the second vowel, as in "orar." It is first necessary, therefore, to learn how to produce the final /-r/, which is a little different from any of the others. When the /r/ at the end of a word occurs before another word, it is just like the /r/ between vowels if the next word begins with a vowel, or the /r/ before a consonant if the next word begins with a consonant. But if the word is final in the utterance, then the final /-r/ is quickly devoiced: that is, the vocal cords stop vibrating before the tongue has stopped trilling. The result is a sort of hiss that resembles an /s/ sound.

3.21.6 SPANISH /-r/

Instructions.—Mimic your model's pronunciation of the following items in pairs, noting the difference between the /r/ between vowels and the final /-r/.

Pronunciation		Spelling	
/-r-/	/-r/		
1	sérâ	sér	sera	ser

Pronunciation		Spelling	
/-r-/	/-r/		
2	dárðn	dár	daron	dar
3	írá	ír	ira	ir
4	pórð	pór	poro	por
5	márð	már	maro	mar
6	flórá	flór	Flora	flor
7	párá	pár	para	par
8	sórá	sór	sora	sor
9	súrá	súr	sura	sur
10	bérá	bér	vera	ver

Spanish final /-r/ is more quickly devoiced if the final syllable is weak-stressed. Note the difference in the following pairs of words.

3.21.7 SPANISH /ᵉr/ and /ᵛr/

<u>Instructions</u>.—Mimic your model's pronunciation of the items in pairs, noting the difference between the /r/'s in final strong-stressed and weak-stressed syllables.

Pronunciation		Spelling	
/ᵉr/	/ᵛr/		
1	rrèbólbér	rrèbólbér	revolver	revólver
2	pàrtír	mártìr	partir	mártir
3	mètér	étèr	meter	éter
4	kànsár	kánşèr	cansar	cáncer
5	àblár	nákàr	hablar	nácar
6	bèktór	bíktòr	vector	Víctor
7	lìbár	bòlíbàr	libar	Bolívar
8	bùskár	àşúkàr	buscar	azúcar

The Spanish /l/ differs from the English /l/ in one important way. In both articulations the tip of the tongue is placed against the alveolar ridge (gum ridge) above the upper teeth and the air escapes around one or both sides of the tongue. But in the Spanish /l/ the back of the tongue is arched high in the mouth while in the English /l/ the back of the tongue drops low. The Spanish /l/ is therefore referred to as /i/-colored—it can be associated with the high-front position of the vowel /i/; the English /l/ is /ɨ/-colored—it can be associated with the central position of English /ɨ/, or even lower.

3.22 ENGLISH /-l/ VS. SPANISH /-l/

<u>Instructions</u>.—Listen to the English word and then to the Spanish word, noting the difference in the sound of the final /-l/. Then repeat the Spanish words

after your model, trying to avoid the influence of the similar English words.

English /-l/		Spanish /-l/	
		Pronunciation	Spelling
1	feel	fíl	fil
2	wheel	hwíl	juil
3	dell	dél	del
4	hotel	otél	hotel
5	tall	tál	tal
6	mall	mál	mal
7	Saul	sál	sal
8	coal	kól	col
9	soul	sól	sol
10	tool	túl	tul

English speakers who pronounce /l/ differently in "steel" and "steely" will probably find the /l/ of "steely" closer to Spanish pronunciation. Spanish /l/ has the same /i/-color in any position in a word.

3.22.1 SPANISH /l/

Instructions.—Imitate your model's pronunciation of the following series of three items, noting the pronunciation of initial, medial, and final /l/.

	Pronunciation			Spelling		
	/l-/	/-l-/	/-l/			
1	líha	híla	híl	lija	gila	Gil
2	lédo	délo	dél	ledo	delo	del
3	láka	kála	kál	laca	cala	cal
4	láma	mála	mál	lama	mala	mal
5	lása	sála	sál	lasa	sala	sal
6	láta	tála	tál	lata	tala	tal
7	lóba	bóla	ból	loba	bola	bol
8	lóka	kóla	kól	loca	cola	col
9	lósa	sóla	sól	losa	sola	sol
10	lúto	túlo	túl	luto	tulo	tul

An incorrect pronunciation of /l/ will mark your Spanish with an "American" accent more than any other consonant sound with the exception of /r/. Though a mispronunciation will not usually cause misunderstanding, it is still very important to try to improve the /l/, since pronouncing it wrong will always call attention to the way you say it and away from what you say.

3.3 | THE VOICELESS STOPS

In English the voiceless stop series of consonants are made in the following way: air in the lungs is put under pressure by the muscles of the stomach and diaphragm; the air column is closed (or stopped) by the lips (for /p/), by the tongue against the alveolus or gum ridge above the teeth (for /t/), or by the back of the tongue against the soft palate (for /k/). When the closure is released, the air bursts through the mouth with an abrupt puff following the /p/, /t/, or /k/. This can be demonstrated by holding a small piece of paper near the lips and pronouncing the words "pill" or "appear," where the /p/ is initial in the word or before a strong-stressed vowel.

The articulation of the Spanish series of voiceless stops differs from English in that this puff of air is not produced; the closure is released before the air pressure in the lungs is built up. As a result the English-speaker, who is used to listening for this puff of air (or aspiration) to help him distinguish the sounds /p,t,k/, may mishear them as /b,d,g/, similar English sounds which are not aspirated.

To produce unaspirated /p,t,k/, an English speaker needs to modify his pronunciation habits to eliminate the aspiration. It might be helpful to practice single words like "palo," by getting set to pronounce the words, then waiting an instant, then allowing the pronunciation to occur in a very relaxed way. By comparing the pronunciation of "upper" (no aspiration) with "appear" (aspirated /p/), this same difference can be heard.

3.31 ENGLISH /p/ VS. SPANISH /p/

Instructions.—Listen to the English word and then to the Spanish word. Then repeat the Spanish words, trying to avoid the influence of similar English words.

	English /p/	Spanish /p/	
		Pronunciation	Spelling
1	pace	pés̩	pez
2	Peru	pèrú	Perú
3	pan	pán	pan
4	par	pár	par
5	poor	pór	por
6	pone	pón	pon
7	pooh	pú	pu
8	plan	plán	plan

3.31.1 SPANISH /p/

Instructions.—Mimic your model's pronunciation of the following pairs of items. Note the lack of aspiration in the pronunciation of /p/ in either position.

Pronunciation		Spelling	
/p-/	/-p-/		
1 pítò	típò	pito	tipo
2 pékà	képà	peca	quepa
3 péchà	chépà	pecha	chepa
4 pésà	sépà	pesa	sepa
5 pákò	kápò	Paco	capo
6 párrà	rrápà	parra	rapa
7 pálò	lápò	palo	lapo
8 pásò	sápò	paso	sapo
9 pátò	tápò	pato	tapo
10 pókà	kópà	poca	copa
11 pórrà	rrópà	porra	ropa
12 pósà	sópà	posa	sopa
13 pútà	túpà	puta	tupa
14 pàƀór	ƀàpór	pavor	vapor
15 pàhón	hàpón	pajón	Japón
16 pàchón	chàpón	pachón	chapón

3.32 ENGLISH /t/ VS. SPANISH /t/

Instructions.—Listen to the English word and then to the Spanish word. Then repeat your model's pronunciation, trying to avoid the influence of the similar English words.

English /t/	Spanish /t/	
	Pronunciation	Spelling
1 ten	tén	ten
2 tea	tí	ti
3 toss	tás	tas
4 taboo	tàƀú	tabú
5 topper	tápà	tapa
6 tone	tón	ton
7 toe	tó	to
8 too	tú	tú
9 tuna	túnà	tuna

Besides not being aspirated, Spanish /t/ is different from English /t/ in its place of articulation. English /t/ is made above the teeth (on the alveolar ridge), but Spanish /t/ is made by placing the tongue against the upper teeth to form the closure of the air stream.

3.32.1 SPANISH /t/

Instructions.—Mimic your model's pronunciation of the following pairs of items. Note the lack of aspiration and the dental articulation in either position.

	Pronunciation		Spelling	
	/t-/	/-t-/		
1	tíkò	kítò	tico	quito
2	típò	pítò	tipo	pito
3	tísà	sítà	tiza	cita
4	témà	métà	tema	meta
5	ténà	nétà	tena	neta
6	tábò	bátò	tabo	bato
7	tálà	látà	tala	lata
8	támò	mátò	tamo	mato
9	tápò	pátò	tapo	pato
10	tárrò	rrátò	tarro	rato
11	tódà	dótà	toda	dota
12	tóhà	hótà	toja	jota
13	tókò	kótò	toco	coto
14	tólè	lótè	tole	lote
15	túpà	pútà	tupa	puta
16	túɏà	ɏútà	tuya	yuta

There is one environment of /t/ in Spanish which needs a special drill: after a strong-stressed syllable and before /-Vn/. A similar sequence in English has a special variant of English /t/ called a glottal catch (or glottal stop). In English words like "kitten, cotton, batten, Latin," etc., the tongue is placed against the alveolar ridge, but remains there for the following syllabic [n̩]; an opening of the glottis (vocal folds or cords) provides the release that is associated with the /t/. These words in English respelling are [kɪtʼn̩, kát'n̩, bǽt'n̩, lǽt'n̩].

In Spanish the similar sequence of strong-stressed syllable plus /t/ plus vowel plus /n/ has no glottal catch articulation, as the following pairs of words show.

3.32.2 SPANISH /⸴tVn/

Instructions.—Mimic your model's pronunciation of the following series of items. Note the articulation of the /-tan, -ten/ syllables.

	Pronunciation		Spelling	
	/tV̂n/	/⸴tVn/		
1	tán	kítàn	tan	quitan

	Pronunciation		Spelling	
	/tV́n/	/⁼tVn/		
2	tén	kítèn	ten	quiten
3	tán	pítàn	tan	pitan
4	tén	pítèn	ten	piten
5	tán	métàn	tan	metan
6	tén	métèn	ten	meten
7	tán	dátàn	tan	datan
8	tén	dátèn	ten	daten
9	tán	bátàn	tan	batan
10	tén	bátèn	ten	baten
11	tán	kátàn	tan	catan
12	tén	kátèn	ten	caten
13	tán	mátàn	tan	matan
14	tén	mátèn	ten	maten
15	tán	látàn	tan	latan
16	tén	látèn	ten	laten
17	tán	rrátàn	tan	ratan
18	tén	rrátèn	ten	raten
19	tán	pártàn	tan	partan
20	tén	pártèn	ten	parten

3.33 ENGLISH /k/ VS. SPANISH /k/

Instructions.—Listen to the English word and then to the Spanish word. Then repeat the Spanish words after your model, trying to avoid the influence of the similar-sounding English words.

	English /k/	Spanish /k/	
		Pronunciation	Spelling
1	kilo	kílò	kilo
2	Kay	ké	qué
3	call	kál	cal
4	Conn	kán	can
5	caw	ká	ca
6	cafe	kàfé	café
7	cone	kón	con
8	coo	kú	cu

Like /p/ and /t/, Spanish /k/ is not normally aspirated, though this restriction is less rigid in the case of /k/.

3.33.1 SPANISH /k/

Instructions.—Mimic your model's pronunciation of the following pairs of items. Note the lack of aspiration in the articulation of /k̜/.

	Pronunciation		Spelling	
	/k-/	/-k-/		
1	kípòs	píkòs	quipos	picos
2	kítò	tíkò	quito	tico
3	kéchê	chékê	queche	cheque
4	kémâ	mékâ	quema	Meca
5	képâ	pékâ	quepa	peca
6	kábâ	bákâ	cava	vaca
7	kádâ	dákâ	cada	daca
8	kápâ	pákâ	capa	paca
9	kásâ	sákâ	casa	saca
10	kóchê	chókê	coche	choque
11	kóhê	hókê	coge	joque
12	kólâ	lókâ	cola	loca
13	kómâ	mókâ	coma	moca
14	kópâ	pókâ	copa	poca
15	kórrâ	rrókâ	corra	roca
16	kúrrâ	rrúkâ	curra	ruca

3.4 | SPIRANTS AND AFFRICATES

The spirants are different from the stops in the following way: the air column is completely closed in the production of a stop but is merely restricted in the production of a spirant. An affricate is a combination of the two; a stop with a spirant release. Thus the affricate /ch/ is sometimes represented by the two symbols /tš/, to show both of the components, a /t/ released as an /š/.

In Spanish, the spirants are normally voiceless, though the /s/ and the /ṣ/ have voiced variants in some positions.

3.41 SPANISH /s/

Instructions.—Mimic your model's pronunciation of the following series of three items.

	Pronunciation			Spelling		
	/s-/	/-s-/	/-s/			
1	sákò	kásò	kás	saco	caso	cas

	Pronunciation			Spelling		
	/s-/	/-s-/	/-s/			
2	súpŏ	púsŏ	pús	supo	puso	pus
3	sótŏ	tósŏ	tós	soto	toso	tos
4	sámă	másă	más	sama	masa	mas
5	sólă	lósă	lós	sola	losa	los
6	sálă	lásă	lás	sala	lasa	las
7	sórră	rrósă	rrós	sorra	rrosa	rros

You will notice that /s/ can appear at the beginning of a word, in the middle between vowels, and at the end. In all these positions the variety of /s/ that is heard in Spanish America (except when the [ʰ] variety occurs, as discussed below) is very similar to the /s/ of most Americans. In Spain, however, there is an obvious difference: the tongue tip is raised toward the gum ridge behind the upper teeth, producing a sound slightly suggesting a lisp. This characteristic of Castilian /s/, more than any other single feature of pronunciation, identifies "Spaniards" to speakers of Spanish from other areas.

There are two important variants of the /s/ described above. It is very unlikely that any one speaker will have both, since only one or the other occurs in any one dialect. The first is a variation of voicing, when [z] appears before a voiced consonant.

3.41.1 SPANISH [s] VS. [z]

Instructions.—Mimic your model's pronunciation of the following pairs of items. Note the voiceless [s] in the first column and the voiced [z] in the second. (C^{vl} means voiceless consonant, C^{vd} means voiced consonant.)

	Pronunciation		Spelling	
	[-sC^{vl}]	[-zC^{vd}]		
1	ĕspósŏ	ĕzbóşŏ	esposo	esbozo
2	rráskár	rrázgár	rascar	rasgar
3	ĕspéltă	ĕzbéltă	espelta	esbelta
4	áskŏ	ázgŏ	asco	asgo
5	dĕskánár	dĕzgánár	descanar	desganar
6	dĕskáná	dĕzgáná	descana	desgana
7	dĕstĕntádŏ	dĕzdĕntádŏ	destentado	desdentado
8	dĕstĕ	dĕzdĕ	de este	desde
9	éstĕ	ézdĕ	este	es de
10	ĕspŏlétă	ĕzbŏlétă	espoleta	es boleta
11	ĕspírrŏ	ĕzbírrŏ	es Pirro	esbirro
12	místŏ	mízmŏ	mixto	mismo

Pronunciation		Spelling	
$[-sC^{vl}]$	$[-zC^{vd}]$		
13 bŭskár	hŭzgár	buscar	juzgar
14 dèstènyír	dèzdènyár	desteñir	desdeñar
15 dìskúrsò	dìzgústò	discurso	disgusto
16 dìspárár	dèzbárrár	disparar	desbarrar
17 dèstìlé	dèzdìré	destilé	desdiré
18 dèspòhár	dèzbòkár	despojar	desbocar

Spanish speakers from some areas, notably the Caribbean, Coastal areas of northern South and Central America, most of the Andean countries on the Pacific Coast of South America, and the River Plate area, have a different variant of /s/, a light [^{h}] sound which appears before consonants and, in most of these areas, at the end of any word. All of the items cited in the drill above would have [^{h}] for [s], since there is a following consonant: [e^{h}póso], [e^{h}bóșo], etc. In all these dialects [s] is retained at the beginning of a word and in the middle of a word before a vowel.

3.41.2 SPANISH [s] VS. [^{h}]

Instructions.—Mimic your model's pronunciation of the following pairs of items. Note any tendency to produce the aspirated [^{h}].

Pronunciation		Spelling	
[s]	[^{h}]		
1 ásǎ	á^{h}pǎ	asa	aspa
2 ésè	é^{h}tè	ese	este
3 pèsár	pè^{h}kár	pesar	pescar
4 àséstò	à^{h}bè^{h}tò	asesto	asbesto
5 désè	dé^{h}dè	de ese	desde
6 rráșǎ	rrá^{h}gǎ	raza	rasga
7 mísǎ	mí^{h}mǎ	misa	misma
8 ásǎ	á^{h}nǎ	asa	asna
9 íșǎ	í^{h}lǎ	iza	isla
10 sántò	è^{h}pántò	santo	espanto
11 sílò	è^{h}tílò	silo	estilo
12 swélǎ	è^{h}kwélǎ	suela	escuela
13 sándǎlò	è^{h}kándǎlò	sándalo	escándalo
14 sùmár	è^{h}fùmár	sumar	esfumar

There are a number of words closely similar in other respects (including meaning), but which have /z/ in English and /s/ in Spanish. The tendency of the English speaker to substitute /z/ is encouraged by the spelling of English, where s often represents /z/. The following list of words is especially difficult.

3.41.3 ENGLISH /z/ VS. SPANISH /s/

Instructions.—Listen to the English word and then to the Spanish word. Then repeat the Spanish word after your model, trying to avoid the influence of similar English words.

	English /z/	Spanish /s/	
		Pronunciation	Spelling
1	Kansas	kánsås	Kansas
2	president	prèsidéntè	presidente
3	present	prèséntè	presente
4	present	prèsèntár	presentar
5	presentations	prèsèntåsyónès	presentaciones
6	visit	bisitár	visitar
7	proposition	própósitò	propósito
8	Santa Rosa	sántå rróså	Santa Rosa
9	Rosalind	rrósålíndå	Rosalinda
10	influenza	imflwénså	influenza
11	Venezuela	bènèswélå	Venezuela
12	reason	rråsón	razón

In central and northern Spain a distinction is maintained between /s/ and /ş/. The latter is an interdental (or more often postdental) voiceless spirant somewhat similar to the initial sound of English "think." The /ş/ has a pattern of occurrence very similar to that of the /s/.

3.42 SPANISH /ş/

Instructions.—Mimic your model's pronunciation of the following series of three items.

	Pronunciation			Spelling		
	/ş-/	/-ş-/	/-ş/			
1	şátò	táşå	táş	zata	taza	taz
2	şèbò	bèşò	bèş	cebo	bezo	vez
3	şépå	péşå	péş	cepa	Peza	pez
4	şá	áşå	áş	za	haza	haz

The items listed below are pronounced alike in most dialects of Spanish but are distinguished in the Castilian dialects.

3.42.1 SPANISH /ş/ VS. /s/

Instructions.—Mimic your model's pronunciation of the following pairs of items.

Pronunciation		Spelling	
/ş/	/s/		
1	áş	ás	haz	as
2	âşár	âsár	azar	asar
3	káşâ	kásâ	caza	casa
4	láşỏ	lásỏ	lazo	laso
5	máşâ	másâ	maza	masa
6	páşỏ	pásỏ	pazo	paso
7	péşês	pésês	peces	peses
8	şwékỏ	swékỏ	zueco	sueco
9	kỏşér	kỏsér	cocer	coser
10	lóşâ	lósâ	loza	losa
11	póşỏ	pósỏ	pozo	poso

In many dialects of Spanish the velar fricative /h/ is pronounced very much like the English /h/ in words like "heel, hoot." Often, however, it is more tense and more forcefully pronounced, with a considerable restriction of the air column between the back of the tongue and the palate.

3.43 ENGLISH /h/ VS. SPANISH /h/

Instructions.—Listen to the English word and then to the Spanish word. Then repeat the Spanish words after your model, paying particular attention to the tense articulation of the /h/.

English /h/		Spanish /h/	
		Pronunciation	Spelling
1	heater	hírâ	gira or jira
2	hurrah	hừrár	jurar
3	holly	hálê	jale
4	harrow	hárâ	jara
5	hoosegow	hừzgádỏ	juzgado
6	Hilda	híldâ	Hilda
7	junta	húntâ	junta
8	aha	âhá	ajá
9	Mohican	mỏhíkâ	Mojica

Spanish /h/ almost always occurs at the beginning of a syllable. In the few words where it is final it tends to drop.

3.43.1 SPANISH /h/

<u>Instructions</u>.—Mimic your model's pronunciation of the following pairs of items.

	Pronunciation		Spelling	
	/h-/	/-h-/		
1	hílȧ	líhȧ	gila	lija
2	hífȧ	fíhȧ	jifa	fija
3	híƀȧ	bíhȧ	giba	bija
4	hékė	kéhė	jeque	queje
5	hálȧ	láhȧ	jala	laja
6	hárrȧ	rráhȧ	jarra	raja
7	hótȧ	tóhȧ	jota	toja
8	hókȯ	kóhȯ	joco	cojo
9	hȧpón	pȧhón	Japón	pajón

The Spanish voiceless spirant /f/ is sufficiently similar to English /f/ to cause almost no difficulty.

3.44 SPANISH /f/

<u>Instructions</u>.—Mimic your model's pronunciation of the following pairs of items.

	Pronunciation		Spelling	
	/f-/	/-f-/		
1	fíhȧ	hífȧ	fija	jifa
2	féƀȯ	béfȯ	Febo	befo
3	fárrȯ	rráfȯ	farro	rafo
4	fókȧ	kófȧ	foca	cofa
5	fómės	mófės	fomes	mofes

The Spanish affricate /ch/ is more lax in its pronunciation than the English /ch/, but it causes no serious problem.

3.45 SPANISH /ch/

<u>Instructions</u>.—Mimic your model's pronunciation of the following pairs of items.

Pronunciation		Spelling	
/ch-/	/-ch-/		
1 chínŏ	níchŏ	chino	nicho
2 chépǎ	péchǎ	chepa	pecha
3 chékě	kéchě	cheque	queche
4 chókě	kóchě	choque	coche
5 chórrŏ	rróchŏ	chorro	rocho
6 chótǎ	tóchǎ	chota	tocha
7 chúpǎ	púchǎ	chupa	pucha
8 chǎpón	pǎchón	chapón	pachón

3.5 | NASALS AND PALATALS

The nasals and palatals offer little difficulty for either of two reasons: (1) they are very similar to their English equivalents, or (2) they are not extensively used to mark contrasts. The nasals especially are like English; /m/ is illustrated below in syllable-initial position.

3.51 SPANISH /m/

Instructions.—Mimic your model's pronunciation of the following pairs of items.

Pronunciation		Spelling	
/m-/	/-m-/		
1 mílŏ	límŏ	milo	limo
2 mítǎ	tímǎ	mita	tima
3 mékǎ	kémǎ	Meca	quema
4 métǎ	témǎ	meta	tema
5 méyǎ	yémǎ	meya	yema
6 mákǎ	kámǎ	maca	cama
7 málǎ	lámǎ	mala	lama
8 másǎ	sámǎ	masa	sama
9 mátŏ	támŏ	mato	tamo
10 móđǎ	đómǎ	moda	doma
11 mólǎ	lómǎ	mola	loma
12 mótŏ	tómŏ	moto	tomo
13 músǎ	súmǎ	musa	suma

Spanish /n/ is similar to English /n/. It can occur in initial, medial, or final position, as the following series demonstrates.

3.52 SPANISH /n/

<u>Instructions</u>: Mimic your model's pronunciation of the following series of three items.

Pronunciation			Spelling		
/n-/	/-n-/	/-n/			
1 nísð	sínð	sín	Niso	sino	sin
2 néƀá	bénǎ	bén	Neva	vena	ven
3 náƀð	bánð	bán	nabo	vano	van
4 násǎ	sánǎ	sán	nasa	sana	san
5 nátǎ	tánǎ	tán	nata	tana	tan
6 nókǎ	kónǎ	kón	noca	cona	con

Spanish speakers from the Caribbean, Central America, Coastal northern and western South America, and parts of Spain, including Madrid, will pronounce the final /-n/ of the third column above like the <u>ng</u> of the English word "sing." This is a normal pronunciation which in general is not considered substandard by other Spanish speakers.

Spanish nasal consonants always show the influence of any consonants that follow them. Only /m/ can precede /p/ or /b/, regardless of word boundaries; a kind of /m/ precedes /f/; an /n/ pronounced against the teeth precedes /t, d, ş, s/; an /n/ pronounced against the gum ridge precedes /l, r/ and, at word boundaries, /y/; an /n/ pronounced against the hard palate precedes /ch/; and a velar [ŋ] precedes /k, g, h/ and, at word boundaries, /w/. The complex statement above simply means that the nasal consonant accommodates itself, in respect to the place of its articulation, to whatever consonant follows, as the following drill shows.

3.52.1 *SPANISH NASALS BEFORE CONSONANTS*

<u>Instructions</u>.—Mimic your model's pronunciation of the following list of items, paying special attention to the nasal consonants.

	Pronunciation	Spelling
1	ùm pókð	un poco
2	ùm pálð	un palo
3	ùm bíchð	un bicho
4	ùm básð	un vaso
5	ùm fókð	un foco
6	ùm fótð	un foto
7	ùm fósfðrð	un fósforo
8	ùn témǎ	un tema
9	ùn típð	un tipo

	Pronunciation	Spelling
10	ûn dátó	un dato
11	ûn déđó	un dedo
12	ûn ṣyégò	un ciego
13	ûn ṣónò	un zono
14	ûn sákò	un saco
15	ûn sénò	un seno
16	ûn lókò	un loco
17	ûn lóƀò	un lobo
18	ûn rríkò	un rico
19	ûn rrátò	un rato
20	ûn ɏérrò	un hierro
21	ûn ɏúnkè	un yunque
22	ûn chékè	un cheque
23	ûn chínò	un chino
24	ûŋ kílò	un kilo
25	ûŋ kóchè	un coche
26	ûŋ gátᴇ̀	un gato
27	ûŋ gá(l)ɏò	un gallo
28	ûŋ héstò	un gesto
29	ûŋ hárrò	un jarro
30	ûŋ wéƀò	un huebo
31	ûŋ wésò	un hueso

The pronunciations of the nasals listed above should not cause difficulties except in the case of the [ŋ] before the velar consonants of words like "gesto" and "huevo," which are given a special drill below. In other cases the patterns of English are sufficiently similar to transfer without special problems. Note, however, that the spelling may be misleading in sequences like "un poco" and "un vaso." The spelling simply does not reflect pronunciation where word boundaries are involved, as the two spellings "tan bien" and "también" show; both are /tambyén/.

3.52.2 SPANISH [ŋ] BEFORE /h/ AND /+w/

<u>Instructions.</u>—Mimic your model's pronunciation of the following lists of items, paying special attention to the nasal consonant [ŋ].

	Pronunciation [ŋ] before /h/	Spelling	Pronunciation [ŋ] before /+w/	Spelling
1	hwáŋ hémè	Juan geme	hwáŋ wélè	Juan huele
2	ûŋ hènèrál	un general	ûŋ wértò	un huerto

	Pronunciation [ŋ] before /h/	Spelling	Pronunciation [ŋ] before /+w/	Spelling
3	ûŋ hénèrô	un género	ûŋ wébô	un huevo
4	ûŋ héstô	un gesto	ûŋ wésô	un hueso
5	ûŋ hérmèn	un germen	ûŋ wéspèd	un huesped
6	ûŋ hèrmànízmô	un germanismo	ûŋ wé(l)ɏô	un huello
7	sôŋ hènèrósôs	son generosos	sôŋ wèsósôs	son huesosos
8	sôŋ hèstérôs	son gesteros	sôŋ wèsúdôs	son huesudos
9	èstrâŋhérô	estranjero	sâŋwiche	sandwich
10	îŋhènyéro	ingeniero		
11	îŋhèrír	ingerir		
12	fráŋhè	frange		
13	tôróŋhà	toronja		
14	móŋhà	monja		
15	îŋhúryà	injuria		
16	îŋhústô	injusto		
17	áŋhèl	ángel		
18	tâŋhéntè	tangente		
19	èŋhèndrár	engendrar		
20	èŋhàwlár	enjaular		
21	èŋhámbrè	enjambre		
22	ûŋhídô	ungido		

One of the few problems occasioned by the English pronunciation of /n/ is the linking of /nt/ in words like "fantasy, twenty," where the syllable division in slow speech would be between the /n/ and the /t/. In normal English pronunciation the sequence /nt/ is realized as a flapped /t/ following a nasalized vowel, so that contrasts in certain stress arrangements are lost, as in:

I want to win her green dress.
I want a Wintergreen dress.

In Spanish the sequence /nt/ is not linked in this way; both the /n/ and the /t/ retain distinct features of pronunciation.

3.52.3 SPANISH /-nt-/

Instructions.—Listen to the English word and then to the Spanish word. Then repeat the Spanish words after your model, trying to avoid the influence of similar English words.

English /-nt-/	Spanish /-nt-/	
	Pronunciation	Spelling
1 canto	kánto	canto

| English /-nt-/ | Spanish /-nt-/ | |
	Pronunciation	Spelling
2 Tonto	tántŏ	tanto
3 lentil	léntĕ	lente
4 junta	húntǎ	junta
5 Tantalus	tántǎlŏ	Tántalo
6 antidote	ǎntídŏtŏ	antídoto
7 quantity	kǎntîdǎd	cantidad
8 Santa Monica	sántǎ mónîkǎ	Santa Mónica
9 Santa Rosa	sántǎ rrósǎ	Santa Rosa

A problem somewhat similar to the linking of /nt/ in English but not in Spanish is the tendency (that English speaking students will carry over into Spanish) to reduce the prominence of /n/ whenever it is followed by another consonant. In English an /n/ in this environment often appears only as nasalization of the preceding vowel. This tendency is not normally present in Spanish, where any such /n/ gets relatively more prominence.

3.52.4 SPANISH /n/ IN SYLLABLE-FINAL, BUT WORD-MEDIAL, POSITION

Instructions.—Mimic your model's pronunciation of the following pairs of words. Note the presence and relative prominence of the /n/ in the first word of each pair.

| | Pronunciation | | Spelling | |
	/nC/	/C/		
1	kǎnsádŏ	kǎsádŏ	cansado	casado
2	kǎnsár	kǎsár	cansar	casar
3	kǎnséra	kǎsérǎ	cansera	casera
4	pěnsádŏ	pěsádŏ	pensado	pesado
5	pěnsár	pěsár	pensar	pesar
6	şěnsúrǎ	şěsúrǎ	censura	cesura
7	kǒnstádŏ	kǒstádŏ	constado	costado
8	kǒnstár	kǒstár	constar	costar
9	gǎnsítǎ	gǎsítǎ	gansita	gasita
10	měnsúrǎ	měsúrǎ	mensura	mesura
11	nǎnsítǎ	nǎsítǎ	nansita	nasita
12	trǎnspǒnér	trǎspǒnér	transponer	trasponer
13	trǎnspwéstŏ	trǎspwéstŏ	transpuesto	traspuesto
14	ǎnsyátikŏ	ǎsyátikŏ	Hanseático	Asiático
15	lǎnşěár	lǎşěár	lancear	lacear

Pronunciation		Spelling	
/nC/	/C/		
16 lánṣáḓa	láṣáḓa	lanzada	lazada
17 lánṣár	láṣár	lanzar	lazar
18 rrónṣáḓȯ	rróṣáḓȯ	ronzado	rozado
19 rrónṣár	rróṣár	ronzar	rozar
20 trónṣáḓȯ	tróṣáḓȯ	tronzado	trozado
21 trónṣár	tróṣár	tronzar	trozar
22 kántȯ	kátȯ	canto	cato
23 ántês	átês	antes	ates
24 dántê	dátê	Dante	date
25 véntá	bétá	venta	beta
26 fwéntê	fwétê	fuente	fuete
27 péŋká	péká	penca	peca
28 núŋká	núká	nunca	nuca
29 béndȯ	béḓȯ	vendo	vedo
30 dándȯ	dáḓȯ	dando	dado

The palatal /ŋy/ is a Spanish sound that occurs initially in very few words, mostly American Indian loan words like /ŋyandú/ "ñandú." It more normally appears between vowels. The /ŋy/ is somewhat similar to the <u>ni</u> in "onion," though the English syllable division is after the <u>n</u>, while in Spanish the /ŋy/ goes with the following syllable.

3.53 ENGLISH /-ny-/ VS. SPANISH /-ŋy-/

<u>Instructions</u>.— Listen to the English word and then to the Spanish word. Then repeat the Spanish words after your model.

English /-ny-/		Spanish /-ŋy-/	
		Pronunciation	Spelling
1	annual	áŋyȯ	año
2	union	úŋyá	uña
3	pinion	píŋyá	piña
4	minion	míŋyȯ	miño
5	spaniel	êspáŋyá	España

There is a sequence of /n/ and /y/ in Spanish which contrasts with /ŋy/ in a few words, though the difference is very slight. The /ŋy/ is pronounced with the middle part of the tongue touching the hard palate just behind the gum ridge, and the /y/ part of the articulation is very short and closely associated with the /ŋ/. In pronouncing the sequence /ny/ the tip of the tongue touches the gum ridge. Both the /ŋy/ and the /ny/ go with the following syllable.

3.53.1 SPANISH /ŋy/ VS. /ny/

Instructions.—Mimic your model's pronunciation of the following pairs of words. Note the difference between them, if any.

	Pronunciation		Spelling	
	/ŋy/	/ny/		
1	ùráŋyò	ùrányò	huraño	uranio
2	àlíŋyà	àlínyà	aliña	alinia
3	míŋyò	mínyò	miño	minio
4	ùŋyón	ùnyón	uñón	unión
5	làbíŋyà	làbínyà	la biña	Lavinia
6	dèmóŋyò	dèmónyò	de moño	demonio
7	èspáŋyà	ìspányà	España	Hispania
8	èspàŋyólà	ìspànyólà	española	Hispaniola
9	èskáŋyò	àskányò	escaño	ascanio
10	òtóŋyò	àntónyò	otoño	Antonio
11	pìŋyón	òpìnyón	piñón	opinión
12	áŋyò	hèrányò	año	geranio
13	móŋyò	màtrìmónyò	moño	matrimonio

The palatal /(l)y/ in Spanish has merged in many dialects with the /y/, the /l/ part of the articulation dropping. The /(l)y/ survives in the upland, Andean regions of Colombia, Ecuador, Peru, and Bolivia, and in Paraguay. It also survives in parts of north-central Spain, though Madrid uses just /y/. The English sequence lli in words like "million, billion, bullion" is somewhat similar to Spanish /(l)y/, though in English the syllable division is "mill-ion," while in Spanish the syllable division is /mi-(l)yón/. Unlike the /ŋy/, the /(l)y/ can occur either at the beginning or in the middle of words.

3.54 SPANISH /(l)y/

Instructions.—Mimic your model's pronunciation of the following pairs of words.

	Pronunciation		Spelling	
	/(l)y-/	/-(l)y-/		
1	(l)yébà	bé(l)yà	lleva	bella
2	(l)yábè	bá(l)yè	llave	valle
3	(l)yágà	gá(l)yà	llaga	galla
4	(l)yámà	má(l)yà	llama	malla
5	(l)yápà	pá(l)yà	llapa	palla

There is a sequence of /l/ and /y/ in Spanish which contrasts with /(l)y/ in much the same way that/ŋy/ does with /ny/. The contrast, however, is even less important, since /(l)y/ has become /y/ in so many dialects, and the contrast even where it is retained serves to distinguish very few words. The following three-way comparison illustrates maximum differentiation.

3.54.1 SPANISH /ly/ VS. /(l)y/ VS. /y/

Instructions.—Mimic your model's pronunciation of the following series of three items.

	Pronunciation			Spelling		
	/-ly-/	/-(l)y-/	/-y-/			
1	bályá	bá(l)y̌á	báy̌á	balia	valla	vaya
2	ályás	á(l)y̌ás	áy̌ás	alias	hallas	ayas
3	ámályá	ámá(l)y̌á	ámáy̌á	Amalia	amalla	amaya
4	gályð	gá(l)y̌ð	gáy̌ð	galio	gallo	gayo
5	ólyð	ó(l)y̌ð	óy̌ð	olio	ollo	hoyo
6	pólyð	pó(l)y̌ð	póy̌ð	polio	pollo	poyo
7	ðlyár	ó(l)y̌ár	ðy̌ár	oliar	ollar	oyar
8	ílyón	mí(l)y̌ón	mí-y̌ð	Ilión	millón	mi yo

In the dialects where /(l)y/ has merged with /y/, the second and third columns are pronounced identically.

3.6 | THE SEMIVOWELS

The semivowels /y/ and /w/ have been partially treated in sections 2.2 and 2.3 on Spanish diphthongs, where their vocalic function was presented and drilled. When the semivowels occur after a vowel in a syllable, they function as part of the vowel nucleus, that is, they are part of a diphthong (as in "ley, hay, soy, aun," etc.); when they occur before a vowel in a syllable, they function as consonants, either as single consonants, as described in the present section, or as part of consonant clusters, described in sections 3.73 and 3.74.

As consonants, the /y/ and the /w/ have pronunciations which vary, both in terms of the particular geographical dialect of Spanish being considered and in terms of the position of the /y/ or /w/ in a syllable or word. This variation is readily noticed in the /y/, which, when it is the first sound in a syllable, may resemble either of two different English sounds, the y or "yess" or the j of "Jess," symbolized [y̌]. When not syllable-initial, this variation is not possible, and the symbol is [y].

3.61 ENGLISH /y/ AND /ǰ/ VS. SPANISH /y/

Instructions.—Listen to the following series of two English words and one Spanish word. Then repeat the Spanish words after your model, trying to produce the Spanish /y/ just as you hear it.

	English /y/	English /j/	Spanish /y/	
			Pronunciation	Spelling
1	yes	Jess	ɏésð	yeso
2	yellow	jello	ɏélð	hielo
3	yea	Jay	ɏé	ye
4	yaw	jaw	ɏá	ya
5	yoe	Joe	ɏó	yo
6	yabber	jabber	ɏábâ	yaba
7	yearn	germ	ɏérnð	yerno
8	Ute	jute	ɏúgð	yugo

Spanish /y/ at the beginning of a word is often considerably more tense than English /y/, but not started as a stop consonant, rather like the /d/ sound, as the English /j/ is. The reason it is sometimes heard as English /y/, sometimes as English /j/ is precisely because it is partially similar to both, but not identical with either; it is, so to speak, between them.

In some Spanish dialects /y/ tends to be more strongly articulated at the beginning of a word than in the middle, even when both are the first sound in a syllable. These different pronunciations of Spanish /y/ can be compared to the medial consonants of the words "major" and "measure." In the following drill, initial /y/ and medial /y/ are compared and both contrasted with the final (semivowel) /y/ which is more like English.

3.61.1 SPANISH /y/

Instructions.—Mimic your model's pronunciation of the following series of three words, paying particular attention to the different pronunciations of the /y/ sounds. <u>ll</u> is symbolized [ɏ] rather than [(l)ɏ] in this exercise.

	Pronunciation			Spelling		
	/y-/	/-y-/	/-y/			
1	ɏá	áɏâ	áy	ya	aya	hay
2	ɏó	óɏê	óy	yo	oye	hoy
3	ɏókê	kóɏâ	kóy	lloque	coya	coy
4	ɏérrês	rréɏês	rréy	yerres	reyes	rey
5	ɏélês	léɏês	léy	hieles	leyes	ley
6	ɏébâ	béɏâ	béy	lleva	bella	bey
7	ɏósâ	sóɏâ	sóy	llosa	soya	soy

If a Spanish medial /y/ is pronounced too weakly, especially between a higher strong-stressed vowel and a lower weak-stressed vowel, it may not be heard. The contrast of the presence and absence of /y/ between two vowels is illustrated in the following drill.

3.61.2 SPANISH /y/ BETWEEN VOWELS

<u>Instructions</u>.—Mimic your model's pronunciation of the following pairs of words, paying particular attention to the pronunciation of /y/ in the second item. <u>ll</u> is symbolized [ẏ] rather than [(l)ẏ] in this exercise.

	Pronunciation		Spelling	
	/V̂V/	/V̂yV/		
1	mía	míẏá	mía	milla
2	bía	bíẏá	vía	villa
3	pía	píẏá	pía	pilla
4	tía	tíẏá	tía	tilla
5	gía	gíẏá	guía	guilla
6	tría	tríẏá	tría	trilla
7	fíó	fíẏó	fío	fillo
8	líó	líẏó	lío	Lillo
9	tíó	tíẏó	tío	tillo
10	bríó	bríẏó	brío	brillo
11	tríó	tríẏó	trío	trillo
12	éá	éẏá	ea	ella
13	béá	béẏá	vea	bella
14	méá	méẏá	mea	meya
15	séá	séẏá	sea	sella
16	béó	béẏó	veo	bello
17	méó	méẏó	meo	mello

Spanish /w/ is similar to Spanish /y/ in the relative tenseness of its pronunciation when it is the first sound in a word. Where initial /y/ suggests /dy/ or /j/, initial /w/ is often heard as /gw/, and a few words are actually listed in the dictionaries with two variant forms, for example, "huaca" and "guaca."

The /w/ is less of a problem for a student than the /y/, however, because it is a relatively infrequent sound in Spanish, especially as the first sound in a syllable.

In the following drill, initial /w/ and medial /w/ are compared, and both are contrasted with final (semivowel) /w/, which is more like English.

3.62 SPANISH /w/

<u>Instructions</u>.—Mimic your model's pronunciation of the following series of three words, paying particular attention to the different pronunciations of the /w/ sounds.

	Pronunciation			Spelling		
	/w-/	/-w-/	/-w/			
1	wá	wáwá	wáw	¡gua!	guagua	guau
2	wákò	áwá	gráw	huaco	agua	Grau
3	wachò	cháwárámá	cháw	guacho	chaguarama	cháo
4	wélá	léwá	háw	guela	legua	jau

3.7 | CONSONANT CLUSTERS

Consonant clusters in Spanish are not nearly as extensive or as complex as in English. They pose certain problems, but they have been postponed until all the individual consonant sounds have been presented and drilled separately. Clusters within a single syllable are sequences of two consonants or, in a few patterns, three.

The two-consonant clusters are most economically described by classification according to the second consonant. Only three types can occur in this position: vibrant, lateral, or semivowel. This is to say, the second member of a consonant cluster will always be /r/, /l/, /y/, or /w/. All these cluster types occur in English (plus many others), though in the case of the clusters with semivowels there are restrictions of occurrence in English not found in Spanish.

Drills on consonant clusters are presented in pairs of words which differ only by the addition of the second member of the cluster. The drill is, then:

$$C^1V- \qquad C^1C^2V-$$

Consonant clusters of the shape /CrV-/ have been partially treated in sections 3.21.4 and 3.21.5. The principal difficulty for a student is the production of a Spanish "flap" /r/ instead of an English "retroflex" /r/, whether as a single consonant or as the second member of a cluster.

In the /Cr/ clusters, only certain consonants can occur, both in English and in Spanish. The consonants permitted in this position in Spanish are the stops (voiceless stops and voiced stop-spirants), the spirant /f/, and the vibrant /r/. In the latter case, only the cluster /rr-/ can occur at the beginning of words, so no contrast in this position with a single /r/ is possible.

3.71 /Cr/ CLUSTERS

Instructions.—Mimic your model's pronunciation of the following pairs of words, paying particular attention to the pronunciation of the /r/ in the second word.

		Pronunciation		Spelling	
		/C-/	/Cr-/		
/p/	1	písá	prísá	pisa	prisa

		Pronunciation		Spelling	
		/C-/	/Cr-/		
	2	péstĕ	préstĕ	peste	preste
	3	pósá	prósá	posa	prosa
	4	páƀŏ	práƀŏ	pavo	pravo
/t/	5	tínă	trínă	tina	trina
	6	téchŏ	tréchŏ	techo	trecho
	7	tátă	trátă	tata	trata
	8	tónŏ	trónŏ	tono	trono
	9	túsăs	trúsăs	tusas	trusas
/k/	10	kístŏ	krístŏ	quisto	Cristo
	11	kémă	krémă	quema	crema
	12	kéđŏ	kréđŏ	quedo	credo
	13	kásŏ	krásŏ	caso	craso
	14	kómŏ	krómŏ	como	cromo
	15	kúsĕ	krúṣĕ	cuse	cruce
/b/	16	bísă	brísă	visa	brisa
	17	bíchŏ	bríchŏ	bicho	bricho
	18	bégă	brégă	vega	brega
	19	bágă	brágă	vaga	braga
	20	bóchĕ	bróchĕ	boche	broche
	21	bóṣă	bróṣă	boza	broza
	22	búskă	brúskă	busca	brusca
/d/	23	dágă	drágă	daga	draga
	24	dámă	drámă	dama	drama
	25	dógă	drógă	doga	droga
/g/	26	gítă	grítă	guita	grita
	27	gámă	grámă	gama	grama
	28	gátă	grátă	gata	grata
	29	gánár	gránár	ganar	granar
/f/	30	fíŏ	fríŏ	fío	frío
	31	fénĕ	frénĕ	Fene	frene
	32	fásĕ	frásĕ	fase	frase
	33	fótŏ	frótŏ	foto	froto

The /Cl/ consonant clusters are more limited, since /l/ does not cluster with

/r/ or with /t/ or /d/ (with the exception of a few relatively recent loan words in Spanish, particularly Mexican place names). As in the clusters with /r/, the only real problem is the proper pronunciation of the component parts of the cluster, since similar sound sequences occur in English.

3.72 /Cl/ CLUSTERS

<u>Instructions.</u>—Mimic your model's pronunciation of the following pairs of words, paying particular attention to the /l/ in the second word.

		Pronunciation		Spelling	
		/C-/	/Cl-/		
/p/	1	pé	plé	pe	ple
	2	pékå	plékå	peca	pleca
	3	pán	plán	pan	plan
	4	pánchð	plánchð	Pancho	plancho
	5	pátå	plátå	pata	plata
	6	pómð	plómð	pomo	plomo
	7	púmå	plúmå	puma	pluma
/k/	8	kísð	klísð	quiso	cliso
	9	kábð	klábð	cavo	clavo
	10	kárð	klárð	caro	claro
	11	kásê	klásê	case	clase
	12	kókå	klókå	coca	cloca
	13	kórð	klórð	coro	cloro
/b/	14	binð	blínð	vino	blino
	15	bédð	blédð	vedo	bledo
	16	bánkð	blánkð	banco	blanco
	17	bándå	blándå	banda	blanda
	18	båsón	blåsón	vasón	blasón
	19	búşå	blúså	buza	blusa
/g/	20	gándê	glándê	gande	glande
	21	gástð	glástð	gasto	glasto
	22	góşå	glóså	goza	glosa
	23	gótónå	glótónå	gotona	glotona
/f/	24	fín	flín	fin	flin
	25	fámå	flámå	fama	flama
	26	fákå	flåkå	faca	flaca

	Pronunciation		Spelling	
	/C-/	/Cl-/		
27	fâtwósô	flâtwósô	fatuoso	flatuoso
28	fóhâ	flóhâ	foja	floja

The consonant clusters which have a semivowel as the second member are more numerous, more complex, and more troublesome. They are more numerous because almost any Spanish sound may be the first member, more complex because they are similar to several alternate possibilities in English; and more troublesome because some of the sequences do not occur in English and others occur only before certain English sounds, a limitation that is not true of Spanish.

Any consonant may precede /y/ in a cluster except /ch, ŋy, w/; also /y/ does not cluster with itself, or with /(l)y/. The sequence /hy/ is quite rare, but occurs in /rrûhyó/ "rugió," /rrûhyéntê/ "rugiente," /sûrhyó/ "surgió," etc.; apparently it does not occur at the beginning of a word in most dialects of Spanish. Other combinations are illustrated below.

3.73 /Cy/ CLUSTERS

Instructions.—Mimic your model's pronunciation of the following pairs of words, paying special attention to the /y/ in the second word.

		Pronunciation		Spelling	
		/C-/	/Cy-/		
/p/	1	pé	pyé	pe	pie
	2	pélês	pyélês	peles	pieles
	3	párâ	pyárâ	para	piara
	4	póchâ	pyóchâ	pocha	piocha
	5	púlâ	pyúlâ	pula	piula
/t/	6	têsô	tyésô	teso	tieso
	7	têsúrâ	tyêsúrâ	tesura	tiesura
	8	téndâ	tyéndâ	tenda	tienda
	9	tárâ	tyárâ	tara	tiara
/k/	10	kén	kyén	ken	quién
	11	ká	kyá	ca	quiá
	12	kóskô	kyóskô	cosco	kiosko
	13	kótê	kyótê	Cote	quiote
/b/	14	bén	byén	ven	bien
	15	bál	byál	val	vial

		Pronunciation		Spelling	
		/C-/	/Cy-/		
	16	bándä	byándä	banda	vianda
	17	báhê	byáhê	baje	viaje
	18	bólä	byólä	bola	viola
	19	búdä	byúdä	Buda	viuda
/d/	20	dȩ̧smár	dyȩ̧zmár	dezmar	diezmar
	21	dȩ̧sméró	dyȩ̧zméró	dezmero	diezmero
	22	dó	dyó	do	dio
	23	dós	dyós	dos	dios
	24	dórítä	dyórítä	Dorita	diorita
/g/	25	gádó	gyádó	gado	guiado
	26	góndár	gyóndár	Gondar	guión dar
/f/	27	fébrȩs	fyébrȩs	Febres	fiebres
	28	férró	fyérró	ferro	fierro
	29	fádó	fyádó	fado	fiado
	30	fárȩs	fyárȩs	fares	fiares
/ş/	31	şéló	şyéló	celo	cielo
	32	şérró	şyérró	cerro	cierro
	33	şár	şyár	zar	ciar
	34	şátó	şyátó	zato	ciato
/s/	35	sén	syén	sen	sien
	36	sérbä	syérbä	serba	sierva
	37	séstä	syéstä	sexta	siesta
	38	sétê	syétê	sete	siete
	39	sámpán	syámpán	sampán	siampán
/m/	40	médó	myédó	medo	miedo
	41	méntê	myéntê	mente	miente
	42	més	myés	mes	mies
	43	már	myár	mar	miar
	44	máhä	myáhä	maja	miaja
/n/	45	nétó	nyétó	neto	nieto
	46	nél	nyél	Nell	niel
	47	nóbyó	nyóbyó	novio	niobio
	48	nótó	nyótó	noto	nioto

		Pronunciation		Spelling	
		/C-/	/Cy-/		
/l/	49	léntỏ	lyéntỏ	lento	liento
	50	lèbrátón	lyèbrátón	lebratón	liebratón
	51	lár	lyár	lar	liar
	52	lásả	lyásả	laza	liaza
	53	lórnả	lyórnả	Lorna	liorna
/-r-/	54	sérả	séryả	sera	seria
	55	bárỏ	báryỏ	varo	vario
	56	nórả	nóryả	Nora	noria
	57	pảró	páryó	paró	parió
	58	mủró	mủryó	muró	murió

In English the cluster /Cy/ usually occurs only before the sound /u/ in words like "pew, cute, butte, few, hue, music," and in some dialects also in "tune, duty, new, lieu." The problem in Spanish is to produce /Cy/, not just before /u/, but before any Spanish vowel (except /i/).

Where Spanish has a /Cy/ cluster, English often has an extra syllable with an /i/ between /Cy/; thus /Ciy/. For example when the Spanish word /àdyós/ "adiós" is borrowed by English, it usually becomes a three-syllable word, pronounced /ǽdiyóws/.

3.73.1 ENGLISH /Ciy/ VS. SPANISH /Cy/

Instructions.—Listen to the English word and then to the Spanish word. Then repeat the Spanish words after your model, trying to avoid the extra syllable which the English words suggest.

English /Ciy/		Spanish /Cy/	
		Pronunciation	Spelling
1	tiara	tyárả	tiara
2	kiosk	kyóskỏ	kiosko
3	Deana	dyánả	Diana
4	Guiana	gyánả	Guiana
5	fiasco	fyáskỏ	fiasco
6	fiesta	fyéstả	fiesta
7	siesta	syéstả	siesta
8	recipient	rrèsỉpyéntè	recipiente
9	patio	pátyỏ	patio
10	labial	làbyál	labial
11	ambient	ámbyéntè	ambiente

	English /Ciy/	Spanish /Cy/	
		Pronunciation	Spelling
12	radio	rrádyỏ	radio
13	idiot	ídyótả	idiota
14	Indian	índyỏ	indio
15	tedium	tédyỏ	tedio
16	tedious	tédyósỏ	tedioso
17	invidious	êmbídyósỏ	envidioso
18	studious	êstúdyósỏ	estudioso
19	compendious	kômpéndyósỏ	compendioso
20	Cassius	kásyỏ	Casio
21	harmonious	ârmônyósỏ	harmonioso
22	alias	ályảs	alias
23	folio	fólyỏ	folio
24	filial	fílyál	filial
25	serious	séryỏ	serio
26	spurious	êspúryỏ	espurio
27	curious	kûryósỏ	curioso
28	glorious	glôryósỏ	glorioso
29	furious	fûryósỏ	furioso

Certain combinations of consonant plus /y/ in English have a history of change to other sounds: /s + y > š/, /z + y > ž/, /t + y > ch/, and /d + y > j/. These changes persist in present-day English as can be seen in the following combinations of English words: /š/ "this year," /ž/ "where's yours," /ch/ "eight years," /j/ "did you." The tendency to make this change can carry over into Spanish if not corrected especially in words of similar shape and meaning.

3.73.2 ENGLISH PALATAL SOUND VS. SPANISH /Cy/

Instructions.—Listen to the English word and then to the Spanish word. Then repeat the Spanish words after your model, trying to avoid the influence of the English palatal sound.

		English palatal		Spanish /Cy/	
				Pronunciation	Spelling
/š/	1	delicious	/sy/	dêlísyósỏ	delicioso
	2	vicious		bísyósỏ	vicioso
	3	malicious		málísyósỏ	malicioso
	4	appreciate		âprêsyár	apreciar
	5	expatiate		êspâsyár	espaciar
	6	mission		mísyón	misión

English palatal			Spanish /Cy/	
			Pronunciation	Spelling
	7	discussion	dĭskûsyón	discusión
	8	confession	kŏmfêsyón	confesión
	9	rational	rrâṣyŏnál	racional
	10	national	nâṣyŏnál	nacional
	11	social	sóṣyál	social
	12	official	ŏfĭṣyál	oficial
	13	militia	mĭlíṣyâ	milicia
/ž̆/	14	vision	bĭsyón	visión
	15	decision	dêṣĭsyón	decisión
	16	elision	êlĭsyón	elisión
	17	illusion	ĭlûsyón	ilusión
	18	confusion	kŏmfûsyón	confusión
/ch/	19	celestial	ṣêlêstyál	celestial
	20	bestial	bêstyál	bestial
	21	question	kwêstyón	cuestión
	22	bastion	bâstyón	bastión
	23	pretentious	prêtêntyósŏ	pretentioso
/j/	24	cordial	kŏrđyál	cordial

In /sy/ column (spanning rows 14–18): /sy/. In /ty/ column (rows 19–23): /ty/. In /dy/ column (row 24): /dy/.

In some cases English words will show both a palatal sound and an /iy/ in words with a Spanish counterpart word in /Cy/. These words, like English "tertiary," Spanish /têrṣyáryŏ/ "terciario," demonstrate additional pressures for mispronunciation.

The fact that /Cy/ occurs in English only before /u/ occasionally has the reverse effect of encouraging students to insert a /y/ in the sequence /Cu/ of Spanish words, especially those which are similar in shape and/or meaning to English words which have the sequence /Cyu/. This is the influence of individual words, since the sequence /Cu/ also occurs in English, in words like "pool, coo, boot, food, moot," etc.

3.73.3 ENGLISH /Cyu/ VS. SPANISH /Cu/

Instructions.—Listen to the English word and then to the Spanish word. Then repeat the Spanish words after your model, paying special attention to the lack of /y/ in Spanish.

English /Cyu/			Spanish /Cu/	
			Pronunciation	Spelling
/p/	1	puberty	pûbêrtáđ	pubertad

English /Cyu/		Spanish /Cu/	
		Pronunciation	Spelling
	2 pure	púrỏ	puro
	3 purity	pừrĭdắd	puridad
	4 putrid	pútrĭdỏ	pútrido
	5 punitive	pừnĭtíƀỏ	punitivo
	6 impunity	ĭmpừnĭdắd	impunidad
	7 popular	pỏpừlár	popular
/k/	8 Cuba	kúƀằ	Cuba
	9 cube	kúƀỏ	cubo
	10 cure	kúrằ	cura
	11 curious	kừryósỏ	curioso
	12 occupied	ỏkừpádỏ	ocupado
	13 oculist	ỏkừlĭstằ	oculista
	14 particular	pằrtĭkừlár	particular
/b/	15 bureau	bừró	buró
	16 bucolic	bừkólĭkỏ	bucólico
	17 butane	bừtánỏ	butano
	18 tribute	trĭƀútỏ	tributo
	19 tribulation	trĭƀừlằşyón	tribulación
	20 ambulance	ằmbừlánşyằ	ambulancia
	21 vocabulary	bỏkáƀừláryỏ	vocabulario
/g/	22 figure	fĭgúrêsê	figúrese
	23 regular	rrêgừlár	regular
	24 regulation	rrêgừlằşyón	regulación
/f/	25 fume	fúmằ	fuma
	26 futile	fútĭl	fútil
	27 future	fừtúrỏ	futuro
	28 fury	fúryằ	furia
	29 funeral	fừnêrál	funeral
	30 refute	rrêfừtár	refutar
/m/	31 mute	múdỏ	mudo
	32 mule	múlằ	mula
	33 muse	músằ	musa
	34 museum	mừséỏ	museo
	35 music	músĭkỏ	músico
	36 mutual	mútwỏ	mutuo

		English /Cyu/	Spanish /Cu/	
			Pronunciation	Spelling
	37	munitions	mŭnĭşyónĕş	municiones
	38	municipal	mŭnĭşĭpál	municipal
	39	immune	ĭnmúnĕ	inmune
	40	simulate	sĭmŭlár	simular
/n/	41	monument	mŏnŭméntŏ	monumento
	42	monumental	mŏnŭmĕntál	monumental
	43	granulate	grănŭlár	granular
/l/	44	salutations	sălŭtăşyónes	salutaciones
	45	salutary	sălŭdár	saludar
	46	emolument	ĕmŏlŭméntŏ	emolumento

The complications of the cluster /Cy/ are matched in complexity and difficulty by the cluster /Cw/. In Spanish, any consonant may occur before the /w/, though /w/ appears in /yw/ clusters only in the dialects where /(l)y/ has become /y/, and /w/ does not cluster with itself. Some combinations are not very numerous, such as /ŋyw/, though occurring in /pắŋywélŏ, bŭŋywélŏ/ "pañuelo," "buñuelo." Other combinations are listed below.

3.74 /Cw/ CLUSTERS

Instructions.—Mimic your model's pronunciation of the following pairs of words, paying special attention to the /w/ in the second word.

		Pronunciation		Spelling	
		/C-/	/Cw-/		
/p/	1	péş	pwéş	pez	pues
	2	pérkắ	pwérkắ	perca	puerca
	3	pérrŏ	pwérrŏ	perro	puerro
	4	pár	pwár	par	puar
/t/	5	tĭnắ	twĭnắ	tina	tuina
	6	térŏ	twérŏ	tero	tuero
	7	térkắ	twérkắ	terca	tuerca
	8	tékắ	twékắ	teca	tueca
	9	tắtúắ	twắtúắ	tatúa	tuatúa
/k/	10	kĭtắ	kwĭta	quita	cuita
	11	kál	kwál	cal	cuál

		Pronunciation		Spelling	
		/C-/	/Cw-/		
	12	kántồ	kwántồ	canto	cuánto
	13	kártằ	kwártằ	carta	cuarta
	14	káhằ	kwáhằ	caja	cuaja
	15	kốtằ	kwốtằ	cota	cuota
/b/	16	béy	bwéy	bey	buey
	17	bén	bwén	ven	buen
	18	bénằ	bwénằ	vena	buena
	19	bélằ	bwélằ	vela	vuela
	20	bárồ	bwárồ	varo	buaro
/d/	21	délẽ	dwélẽ	déle	duele
	22	déndẽ	dwéndẽ	dende	duende
	23	dál	dwál	Dal	dual
/g/	24	gírằ	gwírằ	guira	güira
	25	gásằ	gwásằ	gasa	guasa
	26	gámằ	gwánằ	gama	guama
	27	gánồ	gwánồ	gano	guano
	28	gáchồ	gwáchồ	gacho	guacho
	29	gántẽ	gwántẽ	gante	guante
/f/	30	fĩmồs	fwĩmồs	fimos	fuimos
	31	fé	fwé	fe	fue
/ṣ/	32	ṣákằ	ṣwákằ	zaca	zuaca
/s/	33	sĩtằ	swĩtằ	sita	suita
	34	sénồ	swénồ	seno	sueno
	35	séŋyằ	swéŋyằ	seña	sueña
	36	sékồ	swékồ	seco	sueco
	37	sábẽ	swábẽ	sabe	suave
/ch/	38	chékằ	chwékằ	checa	chueca
	39	chál	chwál	chal	chual
/h/	40	híl	hwíl	Gil	juil
	41	hébẽs	hwébẽs	jebes	jueves
	42	hérằ	hwérằ	jera	juera
	43	hérgằ	hwérgằ	jerga	juerga

	Pronunciation		Spelling	
	/C-/	/Cw-/		
	44 hán	hwán	jan	Juan
/m/	45 mí	mwí	mí	muy
	46 mékà	mwékà	Meca	mueca
	47 mélà	mwélà	mela	muela
	48 mérgò	mwérgò	mergo	muergo
	49 mérmò	mwérmò	mermo	muermo
/n/	50 nébò	nwébò	nebo	nuevo
	51 nèrítá	nwèrítá	nerita	nuerita
/l/	52 lís	lwís	lis	Luis
	53 lísà	lwísà	lisa	Luisa
	54 légò	lwégò	lego	luego
/(l)y/	55 (l)ɏébè	(l)ɏwébè	lleve	llueve
	56 (l)ɏékà	(l)ɏwékà	lleca	llueca
/-r-/	57 . . .	tèrwél	. . .	Teruel
	58 . . .	pèrwánà	. . .	peruana

Most of the above /Cw/ clusters exist in English in such words as "tweed, quit, Dwight, Gwen, thwart, sweet, wheel." As new borrowings like "pueblo" and "Buenos Aires" are generalized, others enter English. The probable difficulties English speaking students will have in Spanish are /fw, chw, mw, nw, lw, ŋyw, (l)yw/.

Where Spanish has /Cw/, English in words of similar shape and meaning have an extra syllable; instead of just /w/ English has /uw/ but with the additional complexity of a /y/ after the consonant and before the /uw/: /Cyuw/.

3.74.1 ENGLISH /Cyuw/ VS. SPANISH /Cw/

<u>Instructions</u>.—Listen to the English word and then to the Spanish word. Then repeat the Spanish words after your model, trying to avoid the extra syllable which the English words suggest.

English /Cyuw/	Spanish /Cw/	
	Pronunciation	Spelling
1 evacuate	èbàkwár	evacuar
2 ambiguous	àmbígwò	ambiguo
3 Samuel	sàmwél	Samuel

| English /Cyuw/ | | Spanish /Cw/ | |
		Pronunciation	Spelling
4	manual	mânwál	manual
5	annual	ânwál	anual
6	tenuous	ténwê	tenue
7	extenuate	êstênwár	extenuar

As suggested just before section 3.73.2, certain combinations of consonant plus /y/ change; /s,z,t,d/ followed by /y/ in the clustering pattern /Cyuw/ become /š, ž, ch, j/ plus /uw/. This change is obligatory in English and therefore exerts a strong pressure on the student's attempts to produce the proper sequence of sounds in Spanish.

3.74.2 ENGLISH PALATAL SOUND PLUS /uw/ VS. SPANISH /Cw/

Instructions.—Listen to the English word and then to the Spanish word. Then repeat the Spanish words after your model, trying to avoid the influence of the English palatal sounds.

| English palatal plus /uw/ | | | Spanish /Cw/ | |
			Pronunciation	Spelling
/š/	1	sexual	sêkswál	sexual
/ž/	2	usual	ûswál	usual
	3	visual	bíswál	visual
/ch/	3	actual	âktwál	actual
	4	mutual	mûtwál	mutual
	5	punctual	pûntwál	puntual
	6	textual	têstwál	textual
	7	perpetual	pêrpêtwô	perpetuo
	8	perpetuate	pêrpêtwár	perpetuar
	9	situate	sítwár	situar
	10	sumptuous	sûntwôsô	suntuoso
	11	fatuous	fâtwôsô	fatuoso
/j/	12	gradual	grâdwál	gradual
	13	residual	rrêsídwál	residual
	14	arduous	árdwô	arduo

There are a number of possibilities for clusters of three consonants within a single syllable. The composition of such clusters is:

First consonant: /p,t,k,b,d,g,f,r/
Second consonant: /r,l/
Third consonant: /y,w/

with the exception of combinations of /l/ as a second consonant with /t/, /d/, or /r/ as a first consonant.

These clusters are exceedingly difficult for an English speaking student, since no similarly composed cluster ever occurs in English. It requires careful listening and flexible performance to mimic satisfactorily the three-consonant clusters. The following drill illustrates those clusters which occur at the beginning of words (all but /bl-/, /gl-/, and /fly-/, which occur within words at the beginning of syllables and are marked with parentheses below).

3.75 SPANISH THREE-CONSONANT CLUSTERS

<u>Instructions</u>.—Listen to each Spanish word carefully. Then repeat each one, trying to mimic your model's pronunciation as accurately as possible.

		Pronunciation		Spelling	
		/CCy/	/CCw/		
1	pr-	pryétò	prwébà	prieto	prueba
2	pl-	plyégò	plwéstì	pliego	Ploesti
3	tr-	tryéstè	trwénò	Trieste	trueno
4	kr-	kryádà	krwél	criada	cruel
5	kl-	klyéntè	klwékà	cliente	clueca
6	br-	bryósò	brwétà	brioso	brueta
7	bl-	(bíblyà)	(àblwéntè)	(biblia)	(abluente)
8	dr-	. . .	drwídà	. . .	druida
9	gr-	gryégò	grwésò	griego	grueso
10	gl-	. . .	. . .	. . .	. . .
11	fr-	fryólérà	frwìsyón	friolera	fruición
12	fl-	(kàntìnflyár)	flwórítà	(Cantinflear)	fluorita
13	rr-	rryésgò	rrwédà	riesgo	rueda

The most likely mispronunciation will be the insertion of /i/ or /u/ before the semivowel to break it into two syllables. The following drill illustrates the pressure of this tendency by comparing English and Spanish words of similar shape and meaning. Note the "extra" syllable in the English word which must not be allowed in the Spanish word.

3.75.1 ENGLISH /CCVS/ VS. SPANISH /CCS/

<u>Instructions</u>.—Listen to the English word and then to the Spanish word. Then repeat the Spanish words after your model, trying to avoid the insertion of an extra vowel before the semivowel of the cluster.

| English /CCVS/ | Spanish /CCS/ | |
	Pronunciation	Spelling
1 expatriate	èspâtryár	expatriar
2 patriot	pâtryótà	patriota
3 illustrious	llûstryósò	ilustrioso
4 industrious	ìndûstryósò	industrioso
5 creole	kryó(l)ẏò	criollo
6 equilibrium	èkìlíbryò	equilibrio
7 congruent	kóŋgrwéntè	congruente
8 incongruous	ìŋkóŋgrwò	incongruo

3.8 **SUMMING-UP OF CONSONANTS**

There are sixteen to nineteen distinct and different consonant sounds in Spanish, depending on which dialect area is being considered. While no Spanish sound is identical with any English sound, all but about five of the Spanish consonants are at least partially comparable to English.

This is not an accurate indication of the amount of difficulty a student might have, however, since there are additional complications in the occurrence of variant sounds: /b,d,g,s,n,y/ each have two major variants depending on their position in a word or in a sentence and on neighboring sounds. The sounds /r/ and /l/ are vastly different from English /r/ and /l/, and the failure to master the Spanish /r/ can occasion serious misunderstandings both in comprehension and in speaking. And the Spanish /rr/ is often one of the hardest features of pronunciation for English speaking students to master.

One area of special difficulty is the way in which Spanish consonants combine in clusters. In spite of the fact that the structure of syllables is more complex in English, there are certain restrictions which do not occur in Spanish, and the pressures of those restrictions must be overcome. The three-consonant clusters in Spanish are all problems because these particular combinations do not occur in English, and the English speaking student must counter the tendency to divide the three consonants between two syllables instead of including all three in one syllable.

One final complication is the fact that the pronunciation of many of the consonant sounds varies from one dialect area to another. Indeed, some areas have as many as three consonants not found in other areas: the /ş/, /(l)y/, and /ŋy/. In general, one Spanish speaker identifies another as being from his own area or from another area largely from clues in the pronunciation of consonants. While the student does not need to produce all these variations, he must be ready to recognize and respond to them.

INTONATION: SUMMARY AND EXPANSION

4

The elements of intonation were presented, discussed, and drilled in chapter 1 in simple pattern sequences avoiding difficult sounds or combinations of sounds. These potential problems have now been separately treated, the vowels in chapter 2, the consonants in chapter 3. We are now able to return to the more complex problems of intonation, with drill patterns that have no phonological restrictions.

4.1 STRESS

Two- and three-syllable stress patterns have already been presented. These are now reviewed and additional patterns of words up to seven syllables are presented. In practicing these words, it is well to remember that the weak stresses are more prominent in Spanish than in English, that vowels are not "obscured" in weak-stressed syllables, and that all syllables—weak-stressed or strong-stressed—are more or less the same length.

4.11 TWO-SYLLABLE STRESS PATTERNS

<u>Instructions</u>.—Repeat each word after your model, working down each column of identical stress patterns.

	Pronunciation	Spelling		Pronunciation	Spelling
	/´ ./			/. ´/	
1	bwénô	bueno	1	mûhér	mujer
2	yélô	hielo	2	rrâhár	rajar
3	báņyô	baño	3	rrâşón	razón
4	rróhâ	roja	4	âƀrír	abrir
5	tárđê	tarde	5	şyûđáđ	ciudad
6	cárrô	carro	6	sêrƀír	servir
7	hímê	gime	7	kôrtés	cortés
8	fáşîl	fácil	8	pêrđón	perdón

Pronunciation	Spelling	Pronunciation	Spelling
/ˊ ˑ/		/ˑ ˊ/	
9 dyáryò	diario	9 ṣerrár	cerrar
10 tyérrà	tierra	10 pèról	perol
11 byérnès	viernes	11 dòktór	doctor
12 dwélèn	duelen	12 mùryó	murió
13 dyúrnò	diurno	13 (l)y̶òbyó	llovió
14 bárgàs	Vargas	14 rrèló(h)	reloj
15 nyétò	nieto	15 fùnṣyón	función
16 chwékò	chueco	16 mèhór	mejor
17 kyérò	quiero	17 rrùhyó	rugió
18 lwégò	luego	18 àbryó	abrió
19 trwénò	trueno	19 lèkṣyón	lección
20 pryésà	priesa	20 fìŋhyó	fingió
21 pwértà	puerta	21 rrìmár	rimar
22 prwébò	pruebo	22 sìrbyó	sirvió
23 pérlà	perla	23 bàyló	bailó
24 klwékà	clueca	24 dùrmyó	durmió

4.12 THREE-SYLLABLE STRESS PATTERNS

Instructions.—Repeat each word after your model, working down each column of identical stress patterns.

Pronunciation	Spelling	Pronunciation	Spelling	Pronunciation	Spelling
/ˊ ˑ ˑ/		/ˑ ˊ ˑ/		/ˑ ˑ ˊ/	
1 rrápidò	rápido	1 tràbáhà	trabaja	1 tràbàhár	trabajar
2 méhìkò	México	2 hàrábè	jarabe	2 nàtùrál	natural
3 fósfòrò	fósforo	3 màŋyánà	mañana	3 àwtòbús	autobús
4 sáŋwichè	sándwiche	4 dìfíṣil	difícil	4 èspàŋyól	español
5 bárbàrò	bárbaro	5 (l)y̶ègádà	llegada	5 rrègúlár	regular
6 déhèmè	déjeme	6 kàmbyábà	cambiaba	6 sàlbàdór	salvador
7 myérkòlès	miércoles	7 byàhéròs	viajeros	7 ùrùgwáy	Uruguay
8 (l)y̶ébèsè	llévese	8 mànéhà	maneja	8 àbùrrír	aburrir
9 báhèsè	bájese	9 sègídà	seguida	9 òlbìdár	olvidar
10 (l)y̶ébènòs	llévenos	10 mòháròn	mojaron	10 àrrèglár	arreglar
11 órdènès	órdenes	11 rrèfúhyò	refugio	11 dìbèrtír	divertir
12 sábàdò	sábado	12 gàrgántà	garganta	12 bèṣindád	vecindad
13 lóbrègà	lóbrega	13 ìdyómà	idioma	13 pèrdònár	perdonar
14 flwórìkò	fluórico	14 èŋkwéntrà	encuentra	14 prèsèntár	presentar
15 fryátìkò	friático	15 gòbyérnò	gobierno	15 kòntèstár	contestar

Pronunciation	Spelling	Pronunciation	Spelling	Pronunciation	Spelling
16 krwórikŏ	cruórico	16 kŏrryéntĕ	corriente	16 lĭbĕrár	liberar
17 mwéstrame	muéstrame	17 wăhákă	Oaxaca	17 ĕntĕrrár	enterrar
18 byátĭkŏ	viático	18 ĭşkyérdă	izquierda	18 ăgryĕtár	agrietar

The four-syllable patterns are more difficult for an English speaking student to master because of the tendency for a medial stress to appear, usually two syllables removed from the strong stress, in English. Thus, for example, "institution, disputation, panorama" have an English pattern /ˏ · ˊ ·/, but "instituto, disputamos, panorama" have a Spanish pattern /· · ˊ ·/. The pressure is, of course, for students to add medial stresses to the Spanish patterns, where they are inappropriate.

4.13 FOUR-SYLLABLE STRESS PATTERNS

Instructions.—Repeat each word after your model, working down each column of identical stress patterns.

	Pronunciation	Spelling		Pronunciation	Spelling
	/ˊ · · ·/			/ˊ · · ·/	
1	préstĕsĕlŏ	présteselo	1	ŏlímpĭkŏ	olímpico
2	búskămĕlŏ	búscamelo	2	ĕstétĭkă	estética
3	kómăsĕlŏ	cómaselo	3	dĭs(ş)ípŭlŏ	discípulo
4	kwéntĕmĕlŏ	cuéntemelo	4	mŏnótŏnŏ	monótono
5	dándŏmĕlŏ	dándomelo	5	mĭlésĭmŏ	milésimo
6	sákĕsĕlŏ	sáqueselo	6	dŏméstĭkŏ	doméstico
7	póŋgásĕlă	póngasela	7	sĕmántĭkă	semántica
8	tómĕsĕlŏs	tómeselos	8	mĕkánĭkŏ	mecánico
9	kĭtăsĕlăs	quítaselas	9	fĭlósŏfŏ	filósofo
10	pásĕmĕlŏ	pásemelo	10	fŏnétĭkă	fonética
11	mwébăsĕlŏ	muévaselo	11	ĕpátĭkă	hepática
12	kámbyĕmĕlŏ	cámbiemelo	12	fănátĭkŏ	fanático
13	dígămĕlŏ	dígamelo	13	tĕléfŏnŏ	teléfono
14	tráygămĕlŏ	tráigamelo	14	sĭmpátĭkŏ	simpático
15	byéndŏsĕlŏs	viéndoselos	14	mŭchísĭmŏ	muchísimo
16	kĭtánsĕlŏs	quítanselos	16	măléfĭkŏ	maléfico
17	óygămĕlŏ	óigamelo	17	tántísĭmŏ	tantísimo
18	dígánsĕlŏ	díganselo	18	băsílĭkă	basílica
19	ábrĕmĕlŏ	ábremelo	19	ăbryéndŏsĕ	abriéndose
20	kántănnŏzlă	cántannosla	20	kŏrryéndŏsĕ	corriéndose
	/· · ˊ ·/			/· · · ˊ/	
1	sămbĕnítŏ	sambenito	1	ĕmbĕlĕsó	embeleso
2	bĭşĭklétă	bicicleta	2	dĕsĕŋkŏnó	desenconó

	Pronunciation	Spelling		Pronunciation	Spelling
3	ĭndĕ$ĕ́ntĕ	indecente	3	mĕlŏkŏtón	melocotón
4	kŏmăndánte	comandante	4	sĕnsăsyŏnál	sensacional
5	ĕtĭkĕtă	etiqueta	5	kŏnstĭtŭ$yón	constitución
6	mĭlĭtántĕ	militante	6	ĭnstĭtŭ$yón	institución
7	dĭspŭtámŏs	disputamos	7	dĕsĕmpăkó	desempacó
8	mŏlĭnĕtĕ	molinete	8	mĕndĭkă$yón	mendicación
9	dŏrmĭtóryŏ	dormitorio	9	dĕsăkátó	desacató
10	dĭs($)ĭplínă	disciplina	10	ĕntŏnă$yón	entonación
11	kŏnŏ$yĕndŏ	conociendo	11	kŏmŭnĭkó	comunicó
12	sŭfĭ$yĕntĕ	suficiente	12	ămánĕ$yó	amaneció
13	pănŏrámă	panorama	13	băsĭlĭkón	basilicón
14	ĭnstĭtútŏ	instituto	14	ĭntĕrrŏgár	interrogar
15	ŏmĕnáhĕ	homenaje	15	ĕntĕrărĕ́	enteraré
16	sŏlĭ$ĭtŏ	solicito	16	fĕrrŏkărrĭl	ferrocarril
17	rrĕstăwrántĕ	restaurante	17	kăswălĭdăd	casualidad
18	ăbŭrrĭdŏ	aburrido	18	ĕŋkŏntrărán	encontrarán
19	$ĕrrăríă	cerraría	19	hĕnĕrădór	generador
20	ăbrĭríă	abriría	20	kărbŭrădór	carburador

In addition to the pattern pressures, which tend to add medial stresses, there are individual word pressures, which usually tend to shift the strong stress as well as introduce medial stresses. This is especially true where words have a similar shape and meaning in English and Spanish, as "constitución, teléfono, carburadór," etc.

The more weak-stressed syllables in a Spanish word, the stronger the tendency to introduce incorrect medial stresses. The patterns below are illustrative.

4.14 FIVE-SYLLABLE STRESS PATTERNS

Instructions.—Repeat each word after your model, working down each column of identical stress patterns.

	Pronunciation	Spelling		Pronunciation	Spelling
	/· ´ · · ·/			/· · ´ · ·/	
1	dĕbwĕlbĕmĕlă	devuélvemela	1	kŏnŏ$yĕndŏsĕ	conociéndose
2	ŏlbĭdĕsĕlŏ	olvídeselo	2	ă$ĕrkándŏsĕ	acercándose
3	ĕŋkwĕntrĕmĕlŏs	encuéntremelos	3	ĕŋkŏntrándŏlă	encontrándola
4	rrĕ$ĭbămĕlă	recíbamela	4	prĕ$yŏsísĭmŏ	preciosísimo
5	ĕŋgrásĕnmĕlŏ	engrásenmelo	5	prĭmĕrísĭmŏ	primerísimo
6	ărrĕ́glĕnŏzlŏ	arréglenoslo	6	prĕsĕntándŏlĕ	presentándole
7	pĕrdónĕnŏzlă	perdónenosla	7	ĕmblĕmátĭkŏ	emblemático
8	kŏntĕ́stĕnŏzlăs	contéstenoslas	8	mătĕmátĭkă	matemática

	Pronunciation	Spelling		Pronunciation	Spelling
9	ȧkwéstȇmȇlȯs	acuéstemelos	9	ȇkȯnȯmíkȯ	eçonómico
	/. . . ⁀. ./			/. . . . ⁀/	
1	prȇsȇntȧṣyónȇs	presentaciones	1	kȯmȕnȉkȧṣyón	comunicación
2	ȧmȇrȉkȧnȯ	americano	2	krȉstȧlȉṣȧṣyón	cristalización
3	ȇkȯnȯmísta	economista	3	ȧrgȕmȇntȧṣyón	argumentación
4	mȯtȯṣȉklḗtȧ	motocicleta	4	nȧṣyȯnȧlȉdȧd	nacionalidad
5	kȯmbȇrsȧṣyónȇs	conversaciones	5	pȯstȇryȯrȉdȧd	posterioridad
6	kȧmȉsȇría	camisería	6	ȧntȇryȯrȉdȧd	anterioridad
7	kȯnsȇrƀȧtóryȯ	conservatorio	7	ȉmbȇstȉgȧdór	investigador
8	lȧƀȯrȧtóryȯ	laboratorio	8	kȧlȉfȉkȧdór	calificador
9	ȉnstȧlȧṣyónȇs	instalaciones	9	ȉntȇrnȧṣyȯnál	internacional

Finally, for practice in manipulation and control, two patterns of longer words are included. Only those with strong stress on the final syllable are listed, since in this position the tendency to add a medial stress or stresses is greatest.

4.15 SIX- AND SEVEN-SYLLABLE STRESS PATTERNS

Instructions.—Repeat each word after your model, working down each column of identical stress patterns.

	Pronunciation	Spelling		Pronunciation	Spelling
	/. . . . . ⁀/			/. . . . . . ⁀/	
1	ȉdȇntȉfȉkȧṣyón	identificación	1	dȇskȧpȉtȧlȉṣȧṣyón	descapitalización
2	nȧtȕrȧlȉṣȧṣyón	naturalización	2	ȉnstȉtȕṣyȯnȧlȉdȧd	institucionalidad
3	kȧpȉtȧlȉṣȧṣyón	capitalización	3	kȯnstȉtȕṣyȯnȧlȉdȧd	constitucionalidad
4	ȇspȇṣyȧlȉṣȧṣyón	especialización	4	ȉmprȇsyȯnȧƀȉlȉdȧd	impresionabilidad
5	dȇkȯntȧmȉnȧṣyón	decontaminación	5	ȧmȇrȉkȧnȉṣȧṣyón	americanización
6	hȇnȇrȧlȉṣȧṣyón	generalización	6	sȕpȇrnȧtȕrȧlȉdȧd	supernaturalidad
7	rrȇkȧpȉtȕlȧṣyón	recapitulación	7	dȇznȧtȕrȧlȉṣȧṣyón	desnaturalización
8	rrȇspȯnsȧƀȉlȉdȧd	responsabilidad	8	ȉmpȇrsȯnȧlȉṣȧṣyón	impersonalización
9	rrȇspȇtȧƀȉlȉdȧd	respetabilidad	9	ȧgrȉkȕltȕrȉṣȧṣyón	agriculturización
10	ȉrrȇgȕlȧrȉdȧd	irregularidad	10	sȕpȇrȧlȉmȇntȧṣyón	superalimentación

As can be seen from the above series of drills, it is quite possible and normal in Spanish to have a series of six (or more) weak-stressed syllables in uninterrupted sequence. A similar patterning of weak-stressed syllables just does not occur in English; two in sequence is possible, three is rare, four unheard of, and more impossible. English structure will not permit extended sequences of weak-stressed syllables; medial stresses are automatically introduced in a fairly regular pattern every two or three syllables.

There are still longer words in Spanish, and variations on the patterns in 4.15, but little can be gained from further, more complicated drill. Even the patterns just presented are of rather infrequent occurrence, relatively speaking. The problem in the long, complex patterns is always the same: correct placement of the strong stress and resistance to the English tendency to add medial stresses.

The tendency to add medial stresses to sequences of weak-stressed syllables in Spanish is a function of rhythm and is therefore not limited to occurrence within a single word. Weak-stressed monosyllabic words, like "el, la, con," etc., when they precede a word, act just like any of the weak-stressed syllables within the word. The following drill shows the influence of the English tendency to alternate strong and weak stresses within a phrase.

4.16 ERRORS RESULTING FROM ENGLISH PATTERN PRESSURES

Instructions.—Repeat each item after your model. Be sure not to overstress the first syllable.

	Pronunciation	Spelling
	/. . ⌣ ./	
1	kòmpèrmísò	con permiso
2	prèsèntárlè	presentarle
3	èŋkàntádò	encantado
4	làsèŋyórà	la señora
5	prèsidéntè	presidente
6	siŋkòmídàs	sin comidas
7	làmùcháchà	la muchacha
8	ìnmìgrántè	inmigrante
9	bàyònétà	bayoneta
10	àdhèktíbò	adjectivo
11	kònsònántè	consonante
12	àspìrínà	aspirina

The tendency to add extra stresses is considerably reinforced when there is a similar English word with a strong stress on the syllable where the stress might be added in the Spanish word. Several of the words in the above drill illustrate this point: "president, immigrant, adjective, consonant," etc.

Some patterns are more readily affected by the existence of similar English words than others. There should be, for example, strong pressure to shift the stress pattern of words ending in "-ción, -dad, -ante, -ente," such as "sensación, ciudad, abundante, absorbente," since in similar English words the stress is on the preceding syllable. For some reason, perhaps because they are so frequent and therefore establish their own pattern in Spanish, students usually have relatively little difficulty with such forms.

Other words, like "doctor, inglés, difícil, español, profesor," have an identical stress relationship, but present a serious problem of correct stress placement. The following drill illustrates a series of words in two pattern comparisons which have proved especially troublesome to numerous students.

4.17 ERRORS RESULTING FROM ENGLISH INDIVIDUAL WORD PRESSURES

Instructions.—Listen to the English word and then to the Spanish word. Then repeat the Spanish words after your model, paying particular attention to correct placement of the strong stress.

English /ˊ · ˋ/	Spanish /· ˊ · (·)/	
	Pronunciation	Spelling
1 telephone	tèléfònò	teléfono
2 acrobat	àkróbàtà	acróbata
3 antidote	àntídòtò	antídoto
4 autocrat	àwtókràtà	autócrata
5 anecdote	ànékdòtà	anécdota
6 figuring	fìgúrèsè	figúrese
7 versatile	bèrsátìl	versátil
8 character	kàráktèr	carácter

English /· ˊ · (·)/	Spanish /· · ˊ ·/	
	Pronunciation	Spelling
1 solicit	sòlìsítò	solicito
2 sufficient	sùfìsyéntè	suficiente
3 imagine	ìmàhínè	imagine
4 deposit	dèpòsítò	deposito (verb)
5 important	ìmpòrtántè	importante
6 expansive	èspànsíbò	expansivo
7 instinctive	ìnstìntíbò	instintivo
8 extensive	èstènsíbò	extensivo
9 policing	pòlìsía	policía
10 immediate	ìnmèdyátà	inmediata
11 preoccupy	prèòkúpò	preocupo
12 democracy	dèmòkrásyà	democracia
13 appropriate	àpròpyádò	apropiado

The tendency in English to alternate strong- and weak-stressed syllables has an important reverse implication. Just as English does not encourage a series of weak-stressed syllables, neither does it welcome more than one strong-stressed syllable in sequence. One way to avoid a succession of strong-stressed syllables in a single rhythmic phrase is to divide the phrase. With the adjectives emphasized, the following English utterance contains four separate phrases: "ten big black bears."

Note what regularly happens within an English word when an ending is added which shifts the strong stress: "advantage" has the stress pattern /· ⸍ ·/, but "advantageous" is /⸍ · ⸍ ·/. When the strong stress is moved to the third syllable, the medial falls not where we might have expected it, as a residue feature of the second syllable, but on the first syllable, conveniently separated from the strong stress by a weak-stressed syllable.

The tendency to avoid two strong-stressed syllables in sequence encourages a distortion where this is a normal Spanish pattern. The distortion is usually a shift of the first strong stress to allow an intervening weak-stressed syllable.

4.18 PATTERNS WITH TWO ADJACENT STRONG STRESSES

Instructions.—Repeat each item after your model, working down each column of identical stress patterns.

	Pronunciation	Spelling		Pronunciation	Spelling
	/· ⸍ ⸍ ·/			/· · ⸍ ⸍ ·/	
1	ìgwálméntè	igualmente	1	lìtèrálméntè	literalmente
2	ùswálméntè	usualmente	2	màtèryálméntè	materialmente
3	àktwálméntè	actualmente	3	hènèrálméntè	generalmente
4	kòrdyálméntè	cordialmente	4	èlsèɲyórlópèṣ	el señor López
5	sèɲyórsánchèṣ	Señor Sánchez	5	àlsèɲyórkástrò	al señor Castro
6	dòktórkámpòs	Doctor Campos	6	ìnmòrálméntè	inmoralmente
7	sèɲyórkástrò	Señor Castro	7	ìmfòrmálméntè	informalmente
8	àsídìṣè	así dice	8	èspèṣyálméntè	especialmente
9	kòlórbérdè	color verde	9	èlkòlórnégrò	el color negro
10	à(l)ɣábyéntè	allá viene	10	èlsèɲyórbárgàs	el señor Vargas

Again it is clear that stress arrangements are a feature of the rhythmic phrase; it is not particularly significant whether the sequence is on a single word or on a series of words, as long as the same sequence of weak- and strong-stressed syllables occurs.

4.2 | SIMPLE INTONATION PATTERNS

It should be possible at this point to introduce patterned arrangements of stress, pitch, and juncture without the restrictions which were imposed on earlier drills on intonation patterns. Consequently, the following drills do not avoid the consonants and consonant sequences which are usually difficult for American students.

Before beginning the drills in the present section, a student might be well advised to review the first section of this drillbook, which was devoted to the elements of intonation—stress, pitch, and juncture—and some combinations of these elements in several simple, frequent patterns. The drills below briefly review and then continue the presentation of additional intonation patterns.

Since most of the drill sequences in earlier drills of this text concern single words, at this time we present a number of symbols and devices that are used more frequently in full sentence utterances, and review some of the symbols that have been discussed in the presentations of single sounds, particularly those used to signal dialect variations. To facilitate reference, they are listed below in tabular form:

/ş/	Not distinguished from /s/, except in the Castilian areas of central and northern Spain, where it resembles the <u>th</u> of English <u>thin</u>. See section 3.42.
/(l)y/	Not distinguished from /y/, except in the Castilian areas of central and northern Spain (but not including Madrid) and upland South America from Bogotá through Bolivia and on to Paraguay. Pronunciations vary, but usually /(l)y/ in these areas is a palatal /l/ and /y/ pronounced in close sequence. See section 3.54.
[b̶,d̶,g̶]	The line through these symbols indicates a spirant pronunciation rather than a stop pronunciation (indicated by the same symbols without the line). See section 3.1. When [d̶] is the last sound in an utterance, it is often dropped, except in northern Spain, where it tends to be identified with the /ş/ of the same area.
[ŋ]	The long tail on the <u>n</u> indicates a velar nasal pronunciation. See section 3.52.2. This sound occurs before /k/ and /g/, as it often does in English, and also before /h/ and /+w/, which it seldom does in English.
/n./	This symbol is equivalent to [ŋ] in the speech of the Caribbean, much of Central America, the coast of northern and western South America, and of some parts of Spain, including that of many people in Madrid.
/s./	This symbol is pronounced like a very soft [ʰ] in the Caribbean, much of Central America, the entire northern and western coasts of South America and the River Plate area. In most of these areas an /s/ before any consonant is pronounced the same way. See section 3.41.2.
[y̶]	When /y/ is the first sound of a syllable, it can in some dialects, notably southern South America, but as a variant pronunciation in almost any dialect area, become a spirant rather than a semivowel. See section 3.61. The [y̶] before a vowel indicates that the /y/ goes with the following syllable and is pronounced as a spirant.
/V̯V/	A small arc under one of two adjacent vowels indicates that the vowel is shortened. It may be a very short independent syllable or it may blend in the same syllable with the other vowel. This shortening is frequent when a word ending with a vowel is followed by a word beginning with a vowel. See section 2.6. Normally when the shortening symbol is placed under a vowel, no intonation dot is placed over it, which implies it is not a separate syllable.
/↓,↑,|/	These are terminal juncture symbols. See section 1.2. The arrows indicate the direction of pitch change as the voice fades out at the end of a sentence. In the

case of /ɪ/ there is no pitch change; and no fade-out when the occurrence is between two phrases of the same sentence. When it occurs at the end of a sentence, there is an abrupt cut-off rather than a fade-out.

These indications have been given for two reasons: (1) to help explain the significance of the symbols in the respelling, and (2) to explain how differing dialects are represented by the same respelling, since any speaker will represent his own dialect area. One native speaker of Spanish will not necessarily agree with another on the small details listed above as dialect variations, and this can be confusing to students.

It is well to bear in mind that respelling is an aid to listening; its object is to point out where the learner should concentrate his attention to hear the important contrasts of the Spanish sound system. Reading the respelling is not a skill that should be required of a student.

The first drill below is a review of several patterns previously presented: information and echo questions answered by normal statements and emphatic (or contrastive) statements. The sentences show one of the frequent and important uses of the /1 2 3 1 ↓/ pattern: to correct something that has been misunderstood.

4.21 NORMAL AND CONTRASTIVE STATEMENTS
/1211↓/ AND /1231↓/

Instructions.—Listen to your model's pronunciation of the following questions and answers. Then be prepared to answer the questions, following the appropriate intonation patterns.

Information question /1 2 1 1 ↓/ and echo question /1 2 2 2 ↑/	Normal statement /1 2 1 1 ↓/ and contrastive statement /1 2 3 1 ↓/
1 dedondes.usted↓	soydechile↓
komo↑ dechina↑	no↓ dechile↓
¿De dónde es usted? ¿Como? ¿De China?	Soy de Chile. No, de Chile.
2 kwantoskwartos.ay↓	aydose↓
komo↑ dos↑	no↓ dose↓
¿Cuántos cuartos hay? ¿Cómo? ¿Dos?	Hay doce. No, doce.

Information question /1 2 1 1 ↓/ and echo question /1 2 2 2 ↑/	Normal statement /1 2 1 1 ↓/ and contrastive statement /1 2 3 1 ↓/

3   dondestaeldokumento↓   esta(l)ya↓

     como↑   aka↑   no↓   a(l)ya↓

         ¿Dónde está el documento?   Está allá.
         ¿Cómo?   ¿Acá?   No, allá.

4   parakes.estecheke↓   paraelbyahe↓

     komo↑   paraelbyeho↑   no↓   paraelbyahe↓

         ¿Para qué es este cheque?   Para el viaje.
         ¿Cómo?   ¿Para el viejo?   No, para el viaje.

5   ketyene↓   tengoambre↓

     komo↑   ombre↑   no↓   ambre↓

         ¿Qué tiene?   Tengo hambre.
         ¿Cómo?   ¿Hombre?   No, hambre.

6   kekyere↓   wiskikonsoda↓

     komo↑   komboda↑   no↓   konsoda↓

         ¿Qué quiere?   Whisky con soda.
         ¿Cómo?   ¿Con boda?   No, con soda.

7   dondetrabahael↓   enlatintoreria↓

     komo↑   enlalabanderia↑   no↓   enlatintoreria↓

         ¿Dónde trabaja él?   En la tintorería.
         ¿Cómo?   ¿En la lavandería?   No, en la tintorería.

Information question /1 2 1 1 ↓/ and echo question /1 2 2 2 ↑/	Normal statement /1 2 1 1 ↓/ and contrastive statement /1 2 3 1 ↓/

8

dondestalapluma↓

komo↑ en.eldormitoryo↑

¿Dónde está la pluma?
¿Cómo? ¿En el dormitorio?

en.eleskritoryo↓

no↓ en.eleskritoryo↓

En el escritorio.
No, en el escritorio.

9

paradondeban↓

komo↑ abeber↑

¿Para dónde van?
¿Cómo? ¿A beber?

bamos.akomer↓

no↓ akomer↓

Vamos a comer.
No, a comer.

10

adondeban↓

komo↑ almorsar↑

¿Adónde van?
¿Cómo? ¿A almorzar?

atrabahar↓

no↓ atrabahar↓

A trabajar.
No, a trabajar.

11

kekyeres↓

komo↑ otraseresa↑

¿Qué quieres?
¿Cómo? ¿Otra cereza?

otraserbesa↓

no↓ otraserbesa↓

Otra cerveza.
No, otra cerveza.

12

dondeaestado↓

komo↑ enlaeskina↑

¿Dónde ha estado?
¿Cómo? ¿En la esquina?

enlakosina↓

no↓ enlakosina↓

En la cocina.
No, en la cocina.

A not infrequent pattern for information questions is one that starts on pitch level /3/ with the first strong stress and gradually steps down to level /1/. This pattern can be represented as /2 3 2 1 ↓/, in which even the weak-stressed first syllable(s) are lifted to level /2/ by the first strong-stressed syllable on level /3/. The special meaning which distinguishes this pattern from the normal /1 2 1 1 ↓/ is importuning or special interest. Thus it is a pattern often used to solicit information from persons one is not acquainted with, say an attendant at an information booth. It seems to be a pattern that marks a question as one for which a serious answer is desired. If the drop were from /3/ to /1/ without passing through /2/, the meaning would be irritation or annoyance. Note the difference in the following minimal pair:

porkemolestas↓   ¿Por qué molestas? (importuning)

porkemolestas↓   ¿Por qué molestas? (annoyance)

4.22 INFORMATION QUESTIONS—IMPORTUNING /2 3 2 1 ↓/

Instructions.—Mimic your model's pronunciation of the utterances in the first column. Then repeat each utterance, raising the pitch of the question word to level /3/, which adds a note of importuning or special interest to the context. The importuning information question is shown in the second column.

Pronunciation		Spelling
/1 2 1 1 ↓/	/2 3 2 1 ↓/ (or /2 3 2 1 1 ↓/)	
1 kwantokwesta↓	kwantokwesta↓	¿Cuánto cuesta?
2 kwantozbinyeron↓	kwantozbinyeron↓	¿Cuántos vinieron?
3 porkemolestas↓	porkemolestas↓	¿Porqué molestas?
4 parakelokyere↓	parakelokyere↓	¿Para qué lo quiere?
5 adondefwiste↓	adondefwiste↓	¿Adónde fuiste?
6 ikwandoseabre↓	ikwandoseabre↓	¿Y cuándo se abre?

Pronunciation		Spelling
/1 2 1 1 ↓/	/2 3 2 1 ↓/ (or /2 3 2 1 1 ↓/)	
7 komolokyeres↓	komolokyeres↓	¿Cómo lo quieres?
8 porkenomedihiste↓	porkenomedihiste↓	¿Por qué no me dijiste?
9 ikwandoselo(l)yebaron↓	ikwandoselo(l)yebaron↓	¿Y cuándo se lo llevaron?
10 dedondemelotraheron↓	dedondemelotraheron↓	¿De dónde me lo trajeron?
11 kwantokwestauntaksi↓	kwantokwestauntaksi↓	¿Cuánto cuesta un taxi?
12 kyen.es.esamuchacha↓	kyen.es.esamuchacha↓	¿Quién es esa muchacha?
13 kestasyendoelmediko↓	kestasyendoelmediko↓	¿Qué está haciende el médico?
14 komose(l)yamalasekretarya↓	komose(l)yamalasekretarya↓	¿Cómo se llama la secretaria?
15 parakesirbelatelebisyon↓	parakesirbelatelebisyon↓	¿Para qué sirve la televisión?

This same pattern is often used in statements that call attention to someone or something, again to indicate genuine interest or concern:

miraesesenyor↓   Mira ese señor.

fihatekomobayla↓   Fíjate como baila.

Both of the patterns mentioned on page 110 (just before section 4.22) end in /↓/: /2 3 2 1 ↓/ information questions—importuning, and /2 3 1 1 ↓/ information questions—annoyance. A similar pattern with /↑/ has an "ingratiating" significance when used with either information or yes-no questions. This pattern is /2 3 1 1 ↑/ (or sometimes /2 2 1 1 ↑/ or /1 2 1 1 ↑/) and can be illustrated in the following sentences:

komote(l)yamas↑   ¿Cómo te llamas?

porkenobyenes↑   ¿Por qué no vienes?

basalsentro↑   ¿Vas al centro?

inotyenes.otro↑   ¿Y no tienes otro?

This pattern is much overused in Spanish classrooms, possibly because it is felt to be very courteous. Actually it is more than courteous; it is almost sugary when used by a man. It is more appropriate for an elderly lady addressing a young boy she has just met than for a normal converation.

Sometimes the pattern is used even in statements and then the undesirable connotations are more conspicuous, as in:

iestespako↑   Y este es Paco.

Because of the limited contexts in which this pattern is appropriate and because of the tendency to overuse it in classroom situations, no drill has been included in this text.

The next drill is designated as "no questions" because of the inclusion of the word "no" in the question. Considered in the light of the anticipated response these could be called "yes or no" questions, since the questioner clearly expects a "yes" in some cases, a "no" in others. That is, sometimes a negatively phrased question in a /1 2 3 1 |/ intonation pattern anticipates a confirming "no" answer; but sometimes, especially with verbs expressing preference, such as "querer, desear, gustar," the same pattern may obviously anticipate a "yes" answer. The two situations are illustrated in English as follows:

No question	Anticipated response
1. Haven't you got the suitcases?	No, I haven't.
(You must not; I don't see them.)	
2. Won't you have a drink?	Yes, I will.
(Of course you will.)	

The intonation pattern is the same as for the yes questions presented in section 1.25. Note the final "terminal-level" or "single bar" juncture, which indicates that there is no pitch drop below level /1/, and that there is a sharp cut-off without fade.

4.23 NO QUESTION PATTERN /1 2 3 1 ↓/

Instructions.—Mimic your model's pronunciation of the utterances in the first column. Then repeat each utterance, adding the word "no" before the verb and replacing the yes-no question pattern with the no question pattern shown in the second column.

Pronunciation		Spelling
/1 2 2 2 ↑/	/1 2 3 1 ↓/	
1 tyenelamaleta↑	notyenelamaleta↓	¿(No) tiene la maleta?
2 aḅlafranṣes↑	noaḅlafranṣes↓	¿(No) habla francés?
3 estuɣalai̯dea↑	noestuɣalai̯dea↓	¿(No) es tuya la idea?
4 kaḅelekipahe↑	nokaḅelekipahe↓	¿(No) cabe el equipaje?
5 tyenes.elcheke↑	notyenes.elcheke↓	¿(No) tienes el cheque?
6 tyeneṇunlapiṣ↑	notyeneṇunlapiṣ↓	¿(No) tiene un lápiz?
7 byenen.embarko↑	noḅyenen.embarko↓	¿(No) vienen en barco?
8 kyeres.untrago↑	nokyeres.untrago↓	¿(No) quieres un trago?
9 legustalaḅitaṣyon↑	nolegustalaḅitaṣyon↓	¿(No) le gusta la habitación?
10 lez̧ustanlozmweḅles↑	nolezgustanlozmweḅles↓	¿(No) les gustan los muebles?
11 deseamashamon↑	nodeseamashamon↓	¿(No) desea más jamón?
12 kyerelmenu↑	nokyerelmenu↓	¿(No) quiere el menú?

Pronunciation		Spelling
/1 2 2 2 ↑/	/1 2 3 1 ↓/	
13 estan.okupados↑	noẹstan.okupados↓	¿(No) están ocupados?
14 ayotros↑	nọayotros↓	¿(No) hay otros?
15 estaẹstuḍyando↑	noẹstaẹstuḍyando↓	¿(No) está estudiando?

The following drill illustrates a pattern where an affirmative confirmation is definitely requested, rather than merely implied, as in section 1.25. This is accomplished by making a statement and without any interruption adding "¿no?" as a tag question on the pattern /1 2 2 2 ↑/.

4.24 AFFIRMATIVE CONFIRMATION QUESTIONS

Instructions.—Mimic your model's pronunciation of the utterances in the first column. Then repeat each utterance on a regular statement pattern, adding at the end the word "no" on a regular question pattern as shown in the second column.

Pronunciation		Spelling
/1 2 2 2 ↑/	/1 2 1 1 ↓ 2 2 ↑/	
1 ezmazgrande↑	ezmazgrande↓no↑	(¿) Es más grande, (¿no)?
2 rresultoḅyen↑	rresultoḅyen↓no↑	(¿) Resultó bien, (¿no)?
3 ɣatyenekasa↑	ɣatyenekasa↓no↑	(¿) Ya tiene casa, (¿no)?
4 traḅahanmucho↑	traḅahanmucho↓no↑	(¿) Trabajan mucho, (¿no)?
5 buskaŋkasa↑	buskaŋkasa↓no↑	(¿) Buscan casa, (¿no)?
6 tyeneznoḅya↑	tyeneznoḅya↓no↑	(¿) Tienes novia, (¿no)?

Pronunciation		Spelling
/1 2 2 2 ↑/	/1 2 1 1	2 2 ↑/	
7 ablarrapido↑	ablarrapido|no↑	(¿) Habla rápido, (¿no)?
8 asikree↑	asikree|no↑	(¿) Así cree, (¿no)?
9 byenemastarde↑	byenemastarde|no↑	(¿) Viene más tarde, (¿no)?
10 labalarropa↑	labalarropa|no↑	(¿) Lava la ropa, (¿no)?
11 kwidalozninyoz↑	kwidalozninyoz|no↑	(¿) Cuid a los niños, (¿no)?
12 kyeres.agwa↑	kyeres.agwa|no↑	(¿) Quieres agua, (¿no)?
13 deseamas.sopa↑	deseamas.sopa|no↑	(¿) Desea más sopa, (¿no)?
14 estamozlistos↑	estamozlistos|no↑	(¿) Estamos listos, (¿no)?
15 bakantar↑	bakantar|no↑	(¿) Va a cantar, (¿no)?

There are also, of course, negative confirmation questions. They are similar to those above, but have the negative particle "no" before the verb and use "¿verdad?" as the tag question, shortened from the longer "¿no es verdad?"

4.25 NEGATIVE CONFIRMATION QUESTIONS

Instructions.—Mimic your model's pronunciation of the utterances in the first column. Then add "no" before the verb and repeat each utterance on a regular statement pattern, adding at the end the word "¿verdad?" on a regular question pattern as shown in the second column.

Pronunciation		Spelling
/1 2 2 2 ↑/	/1 2 1 1	1 2 2 ↑/	
1 balelapena↑	nobalelapena|berdad↑	(¿) (No) vale la pena, (¿verdad)?

Pronunciation		Spelling
/1 2 2 2 ↑/	/1 2 1 1 ǀ 1 2 2 ↑/	
2 ezmuykaro↑	noezmuykaro ǀ berdad↑	(¿) (No) es muy caro, (¿verdad)?
3 tyenedormitoryo↑	notyenedormitoryo ǀ berdad↑	(¿) (No) tiene dormitorio, (¿verdad)?
4 baylanmucho↑	nobaylanmucho ǀ berdad↑	(¿) (No) bailan mucho, (¿verdad)?
5 byenemaŋyana↑	nobyenemaŋyana ǀ berdad↑	(¿) (No) viene mañana, (¿verdad)?
6 bas.alaboda↑	nobas.alaboda ǀ berdad↑	(¿) (No) vas a la boda, (¿verdad)?
7 sedapropina↑	nosedapropina ǀ berdad↑	(¿) (No) se da propina, (¿verdad)?
8 seaseptachekes↑	noseaseptachekes ǀ berdad↑	(¿) (No) se acepta cheques, (¿verdad)?
9 estatrabahando↑	noestatrabahando ǀ berdad↑	(¿) (No) está trabajando, (¿verdad)?
10 estaskontenta↑	noestaskontenta ǀ berdad↑	(¿) (No) estás contenta, (¿verdad)?
11 lezlos.anunsyos↑	nolezlos.anunsyos ǀ berdad↑	(¿) (No) lees los anuncios, (¿verdad)?
12 debenmucho↑	nodebenmucho ǀ berdad↑	(¿) (No) deben mucho, (¿verdad)?
13 tegustalaensalada↑	notegustalaensalada ǀ berdad↑	(¿) (No) te gusta la ensalada, (¿verdad)?

Pronunciation		Spelling
/1 2 2 2 ↑/	/1 2 1 1 ǀ 1 2 2 ↑/	
14 kyereͅagwamineral↑	nokyereͅ ǀ agwamineral ǀ berbad↑	(¿) (No) quiere agua mineral, (¿verdad)?
15 akibendenrrebistas↑	akinobenden ǀ rrebistas ǀ berdad↑	(¿) Aquí (no) venden revistas, (¿verdad)?

Echo questions are a kind of contrastive utterance, repeated because they were not heard or not understood when first asked. They are normally pronounced on an emphatic (or contrastive) pattern: /1 2 3 1 ↓/. In addition to the change from a normal to contrastive intonation pattern, the words "que si" are added before a yes-no question; they are roughly equivalent to "I said" in the repeated question, "I said, can we see him now?"

4.26 YES-NO ECHO QUESTIONS

Instructions.—Mimic your model's pronunciation of the utterances in the first column. Then add "que si" and repeat each question on the contrastive pattern /1 2 3 1 ↓/. The echo question is shown in the second column.

Pronunciation		Spelling
/1 2 2 2 ↑/	/1 2 3 1 ↓/	
1 podemozberlo↑	kesipodemozberlo↓	¿(Que si) podemos verlo?
2 legustalabitasyon↑	kesilegustalabitasyon↓	¿(Que si) le gusta la habitación?
3 sonmuyrrigorosos↑	kesisonmuyrrigorosos↓	¿(Que si) son muy rigorosos?
4 akabandesalir↑	kesiakabandesalir↓	¿(Que si) acaban de salir?
5 es.e(l)yasoltera↑	kesies.e(l)yasoltera↓	¿(Que si) es ella soltera?
6 ban.alͣentro↑	kesiban.alͣentro↓	¿(Que si) van al centro?
7 bibes.en.un.otel↑	kesibibes.en.un.otel↓	¿(Que si) vives en un hotel?

Pronunciation		Spelling
/1 2 2 2 ↑/	/1 2 3 1 ↓/	
8 estaọkupado↑	kesiẹstaọkupado↓	¿(Que si) está ocupado?
9 tyenes.otro↑	kesityenes.otro↓	¿(Que si) tienes otro?
10 bas.alṣentro↑	kesibas.alṣentro↓	¿(Que si) vas al centro?
11 estaṣyerto↑	kesiẹstaṣyerto↓	¿(Que si) está cierto?
12 kyerekonsultarle↑	kesikyerekonsultarle↓	¿(Que si) quiere consultarle?
13 son.estazmaletas↑	kesison.estazmaletas↓	¿(Que si) son estas maletas?
14 bamos.akomeraora↑	kesibamos.akomeraora↓	¿(Que si) vamos a comer ahora?
15 balelapenạir↑	kesibalelapenạir↓	¿(Que si) vale la pena ir?

The pattern for information echo questions is identical, though the pattern of the original question is, of course, different. Also just "que," rather than "que si," is added at the beginning of the echo question.

4.26.1 INFORMATION ECHO QUESTIONS

Instructions.—Mimic your model's pronunciation of the utterances in the first column. Then add "que" and repeat each question on the contrastive pattern /1 2 3 1 ↓/. The echo question is shown in the second column.

Pronunciation		Spelling
/1 2 1 1 ↓/	/1 2 3 1 ↓/	
1 kwantoledebo↓	kekwantoledebo↓	¿(Que) cuánto le debo?
2 dedondes.usted↓	kededondes.usted↓	¿(Que) de dónde es usted?

Pronunciation		Spelling
/1 2 1 1 ↓/	/1 2 3 1 ↓/	
3 akẹoraba↓	kẹakẹoraba↓	¿(Que) a qué hora va?
4 kwandoseba↓	kekwandoseba↓	¿(Que) cuándo se va?
5 dekekolor↓	kedekekolor↓	¿(Que) de qué color?
6 eŋkwantolobende↓	keŋkwantolobende↓	¿(Que) en cuánto lo vende?
7 porkenokyeres↓	keporkenokyeres↓	¿(Que) por qué no quieres?
8 kwandolọarreglan↓	kekwandolọarreglan↓	¿(Que) cuándo lo arreglan?
9 komolokyeres↓	kekomolokyeres↓	¿(Que) cómo lo quieres?
10 parakebyenen↓	keparakebyenen↓	¿(Que) para qué vienen?
11 paradondeba↓	keparadondeba↓	¿(Que) para dónde va?
12 dondestapepe↓	kedondestapepe↓	¿(Que) dónde está Pepe?
13 kwantos.oteles.ay↓	kekwantos.oteles.ay↓	¿(Que) cuántos hoteles hay?
14 dondestalahensya↓	kedondestalahensya↓	¿(Que) dónde está la agencia?
15 kyen.es.esaseŋyorita↓	kekyen.es.esaseŋyorita↓	¿(Que) quién es esa señorita?

When two yes-no questions are combined in such a way that the expected answer is one alternative or the other, the combination is called a choice question. The following drill is an exercise in making a choice question from two yes-no questions. Note that a choice question must be uttered in two phrases, and that the second must end in /↓/; otherwise the result is just a more complex yes-no question. If, for example, the question is "Do you want cake or ice cream for dessert?" and the final juncture is /↑/, the appropriate answer would be "No" or "Yes, either one." The occurrence of /↑/ after "cake" and /↓/ after "ice cream" means that the person is asking for a choice between the two.

Note also that when the two questions are combined in a single question, an automatic contrast is established between the two items that make up the choice. The result is that the pitch rise to level /2/ in the first phrase will occur not necessarily on the first strong-stressed syllable but on the one in the word which is to be contrasted. Consequently the /1 2 2 2 ↑/ pattern of the first yes-no question becomes /1 1 2 2 ↑/ as the first phrase of the longer choice question. This is a very common intonation pattern for choice questions, though of course not the only one that is used.

4.27 CHOICE QUESTIONS

Instructions.—Mimic your model's pronunciation of the utterances in the first two columns. Then combine the two, substituting "o" for the second occurrence of the verb, making the pitch change (up in the first phrase and down in the second) on the items in contrast and substituting /↓/ for /↑/ after the second phrase. The choice question is shown in the third column.

/1 2 2 2 ↑/	/1 2 2 2 ↑/	/1 1 2 2 ↑ 2 2 1 1 ↓/
1 dalaka(l)ye↑	dalpatyo↑	dalaka(l)ye↑ ọalpatyo↓
		¿Da a la calle, o al patio?
2 imbitalhefe↑	imbitasus.amigos↑	imbitalhefe↑ ọasus.amigos↓
		¿Invita al jefe, o a sus amigos?
3 empeṣoạlas.seys↑	empeṣoạlas.syete↑	empeṣoạlas.seys↑ ọalas.syete↓
		¿Empezó a las seis, o a las siete?
4 lachikạesfea↑	lachikạezbonita↑	lachikạesfea↑ obonita↓
		¿La chica es fea, o bonita?
5 komemos.aki↑	komemos.a(l)ỹi↑	komemos.aki↑ ọa(l)ỹi↓
		¿Comemos aquí, o allí?
6 (l)ỹegoạyer↑	(l)ỹegoantyer↑	(l)ỹegoạyer↑ ọantyer↓
		¿Llegó ayer, o antier?

/1 2 2 2 ↑/	/1 2 2 2 ↑/	/1 1 2 2 ↑ 2 2 1 1 ↓/
7 sebamaŋyana↑	sebapasadomaŋyana↑	sebamaŋyana↑ opasadomaŋyana↓ ¿Se va mañana, o pasado mañana?
8 pronunsyambyen↑	pronunsyanmal↑	pronunsyambyen↑ omal↓ ¿Pronuncian bien, o mal?
9 lefaltandos↑	lefaltantres↑	lefaltandos↑ otres↓ ¿Le faltan dos o tres?
10 iŋkluyenlalus↑	iŋkluyen.elagwa↑	iŋkluyenlalus↑ oelagwa↓ ¿Incluyen la luz, o el agua?
11 byenellunes↑	byenelmartes↑	byenellunes↑ oelmartes↓ ¿Viene el lunes, o el martes?
12 baylazmucho↑	baylaspoko↑	baylazmucho↑ opoko↓ ¿Bailas mucho, o poco?
13 bamos.alparke↑	bamos.almuseo↑	bamos.alparke↑ oalmuseo↓ ¿Vamos al parque, o al museo?
14 estudyofranses↑	estudyoespaŋyol↑	estudyofranses↑ oespaŋyol↓ ¿Estudió francés o español?
15 byenemporabyon↑	byenemporbarko↑	byenemporabyon↑ oporbarko↓ ¿Vienen por avión, o por barco?

The next drill is designed to show the pattern change from "normal" to "deliberate." This change is made by dividing one phrase into two shorter phrases by inserting /|/ in the appropriate place.

The relative length of intonation phrases indicates style of speaking; in slow, formal speech the intonation phrases are shorter (there tend to be more /|/'s breaking up sentences)—in faster, conversational speech the intonation phrases are longer (there are fewer /|/'s in the sentences).

There are extremes in both directions, phrases too long or too short, neither of which represents normal conversation. A poor reader may pronounce each word, or even each syllable, as a separate intonation phrase—Mr. Winchell succeeds in saying something like "Good evening Mr. and Mrs. America and all the ships at sea" as a single intonation phrase. Between the extremes there is still a latitude that can be considered normal. The variations in the following drill are well within that latitude.

One might legitimately ask what the features of /|/ are and how this "medial" juncture is recognized or identified. Roughly speaking, it is the place in the sentence which a native speaker feels to be a potential pause point. There is a measure of slowing down during the last heavier-stressed syllable before /|/ and often, though not necessarily always, a drop in pitch on the first syllable after it.

As suggested above, this juncture cannot occur just anywhere in a sentence. The juncture of course should not be confused with hesitation pause. In general, words most closely related to each other in the formation of the sentence are least likely to be divided by /|/. Note the possible divisions of the following English sentence:

One phrase:	The captain is the one.
Two phrases:	The captain | is the one.
	The captain is | the one.
Three phrases:	The captain | is | the one.

As one phrase this sentence is perfectly normal, probably spoken with "captain" and "is" contracted. It is more deliberate as two phrases, and very deliberate as three, probably spoken with lots of emphasis on "captain," "is," and "one." Any further division, however, by the addition of /|/ anywhere else in the sentence, would not be normal spoken English.

4.28 DELIBERATE—WITH PITCH DROP AFTER /|/

Instructions.—Mimic your model's pronunciation of the utterances in the first column. Then repeat each utterance, adding a single bar juncture with a following pitch drop, as shown in the second column.

Pronunciation		Spelling
/1 2 1 1 ↓/	/1 2 2 2 | 1 1 2 1 ↓/	
1 bamos.alaembahada↓	bamos|alaembahada↓	Vamos a la embajada.
2 yasonlas.ocho↓	yason|las.ocho↓	Ya son las ocho.
3 elmioezrroho↓	elmio|ezrroho↓	El mío es rojo.
4 mariaeskasada↓	maria|eskasada↓	María es casada.

Pronunciation		Spelling
/1 2 1 1 ↓/	/1 2 2 2 │ 1 1 2 1 ↓/	
5 elotroestaki↓	elotro│estaki↓	El otro está aquí.
6 sefweron.asedias↓	sefweron│asedias↓	Se fueron hace días.
7 keremozdesirselo↓	keromoz│desirselo↓	Queremos decírselo.
8 ablakonlasenyorita↓	abla│konlasenyorita↓	Habla con la señorita.
9 (l)yegaronkontentos↓	(l)yegaron│kontentos↓	Llegaron contentos.
10 manyanaempesamos↓	manyana│empesamos↓	Mañana empezamos.
11 yabyenemolina↓	yabyene│molina↓	Ya viene Molina.
12 pasemellibro↓	paseme│ellibro↓	Páseme el libro.
13 prestemelapluma↓	presteme│lapluma↓	Présteme la pluma.
14 aialaiskyerda↓	ai│alaiskyerda↓	Ahí a la izquierda.
15 trabahankon.nosotros↓	trabahan│kon.nosotros↓	Trabajan con nosotros.

The next drill is an example of dividing one intonation phrase into two without a pitch drop after /│/. The feature that identifies the insertion is a lengthening of the strong-stressed syllable preceding /│/.

4.28.1 DELIBERATE—WITH NO PITCH DROP AFTER /│/

Instructions.—Mimic your model's pronunciation of the utterances in the first column. Then repeat the utterance, adding a single bar juncture, as shown in the second column.

	Pronunciation		Spelling
	/1 2 1 1 ↓/	/1 2 2 2 ǀ 2 2 1 1 ↓/	
1	bamos.al̯aembahada↓	bamos ǀ al̯aembahada↓	Vamos a la embajada.
2	ɏasonlas.ocho↓	ɏason ǀ las.ocho↓	Ya son las ocho.
3	elmi̯oezrroho↓	elmio ǀ ezrroho↓	El mío es rojo.
4	mari̯aeskasada↓	maria ǀ eskasada↓	María es casada.
5	elotro̯estaki↓	elotro ǀ estaki↓	El otro está aquí.
6	sefweron.as̯edias↓	sefweron ǀ as̯edias↓	Se fueron hace días.
7	keremozdes̯irselo↓	keremoz ǀ des̯irselo↓	Queremos decírselo.
8	aᵬlakonlaseɲyorita↓	aᵬla ǀ konlaseɲyorita↓	Habla con la señorita.
9	(l)ɏegaroŋkontentos↓	(l)ɏegaroŋ ǀ kontentos↓	Llegaron contentos.
10	maɲyan̯aempes̬amos↓	maɲyana ǀ empes̬amos↓	Mañana empezamos.
11	ɏaᵬyenemolina↓	ɏaᵬyene ǀ molina↓	Ya viene Molina.
12	pasemelliᵬro↓	paseme ǀ elliᵬro↓	Páseme el libro.
13	prestemelapluma↓	presteme ǀ lapluma↓	Présteme la pluma.
14	ai̯al̯ai̯skyerda↓	ai ǀ al̯ai̯skyerda↓	Ahí a la izquierda.
15	traᵬahaŋkon.nosotros↓	traᵬahaŋ ǀ kon.nosotros↓	Trabajan con nosotros.

The two patterns illustrated above are undoubtedly not the only specific changes that can occur when speech is slowed down, but they are samples of the <u>kinds</u> of changes that occur. Also they give an insight into the patterns of longer, more complex sentences, spoken deliberately or at normal speed.

We turn now to examples of specific English influence which conflict with Spanish patterns in similar types of sentences. Some of these comparisons have already been made: English normal statement /2 3 1 ↓/ resembles Spanish emphatic or contrastive statement /1 2 3 1 ↓/; Spanish normal statement /1 2 1 1 ↓/ resembles a pattern that expresses boredom or brusqueness /2 1 1 ↓/ in English. English yes-no questions /2 3 3 ↑/ rise somewhat higher than Spanish /1 2 2 2 ↑/, although there is relatively little undesirable carry-over in the last case.

The following two drills represent pattern comparisons that have rather serious consequences, since a carry-over from either language to the other gives results that range from misleading to ludicrous. The first group represents a pattern that might be called "sentence modifiers"; they include mainly vocatives (the names of people spoken to) and some adverbs. The proper Spanish pattern /1 1 1 1 ↓/ is avoided by English speakers because it is used only to show a marked status difference in social standing, as when a soldier standing at attention says "Yes, sir" to an officer. Yet the English pattern /2 2 2 ↑/ sounds strange, almost effeminate in Spanish.

4.29 ERRORS RESULTING FROM SPECIFIC ENGLISH INFLUENCE—SENTENCE MODIFIERS

<u>Instructions</u>.—Listen to the English sentence and then to the Spanish sentence. Then repeat the Spanish sentences after your model, paying particular attention to the proper intonation of the sentence modifier.

English /... | 2 2 2 ↑/	Pronunciation /... | 1 1 1 1 ↓/	Spelling
1 Good morning, sir.	bwenozdias | seŋyor↓	Buenos días, señor.
2 Good afternoon, ma'am.	bwenastardes | seŋyora↓	Buenas tardes, señora.
3 Good evening, miss.	bwenaznoches | seŋyorita↓	Buenas noches, señorita.
4 Good morning, Mr. Alvarez.	bwenozdias | seŋyoralbares↓	Buenos días, Señor Alvarez.
5 Come in, Mr. Gomez.	paseadelante | seŋyorgomes↓	Pase adelante, Señor Gómez.

English /... | 2 2 2 ↑/	Pronunciation /... | 1 1 1 ↓/	Spelling
6 Come in, Miss Vargas.	pase | señoritabargas↓	Pase, Señorita Vargas.
7 Come in, Mrs. Herrera.	adelante | señoraerrera↓	Adelante, Señora Herrera.
8 It's fine, Miss Rodriguez.	estabyen | señoritarrodriges↓	Está bien, Señorita Rodríguez.
9 Of course, Mary.	porsupwesto | maria↓	Por supuesto, María.
10 I can't now, Juanita.	aoranopwedo | hwanita↓	Ahora no puedo, Juanita.
11 I'm sorry, Paul.	losyento | pablo↓	Lo siento, Pablo.
12 Very well, thank you.	muybyeŋ | grasyas↓	Muy bien, gracias.
13 Same here, thank you.	igwalmente | grasyas↓	Igualmente, gracias.
14 Yes, Mr. Campos.	si | señorkampos↓	Sí, Señor Campos.
15 No, thank you.	No | grasyas↓	No, gracias.

The other pattern where there is a considerable and important difference is in expressions of leavetaking. English has a special pattern /2 3 2 ↑/, which is unlike any common pattern in Spanish. When carried over into Spanish, it is perplexingly inappropriate, often with implications of insincerity.

4.29.1 ERRORS RESULTING FROM SPECIFIC ENGLISH INFLUENCE—LEAVETAKINGS

Instructions.—Listen to the English sentence and then to the Spanish sentence. Then repeat the Spanish sentences after your model, paying particular attention to the proper intonation.

English /2 3 2 ↑/	Pronunciation /1 1 2 1 ↓/	Spelling
1 See you tomorrow.	astamaṇyana↓	Hasta mañana.
2 See you later.	astalwego↓	Hasta luego.
3 Be seeing you.	astalabista↓	Hasta la vista.
4 See you this afternoon.	astạestatarde↓	Hasta esta tarde.
5 See you Monday.	astạellunes↓	Hasta el lunes.
6 See you at seven.	astalas.syete↓	Hasta las siete.
7 Good luck.	bwenaswerte↓	Buena suerte.
8 Have a nice trip.	bwembyahe↓	Buen viaje.
9 Hope you sleep well.	kedwermabyen↓	Que duerma bien.
10 Hope you make out OK.	kelebayabyen↓	Que le vaya bien.
11 Glad to have met you.	muchogustodekonoṣerlo↓	Mucho gusto de conocerlo.
12 It's been nice talking to you.	muchogustodeoirlo↓	Mucho gusto de oirlo.
13 Well, I gotta go now.	pwez|yameboy↓	Pues, ya me voy.
14 Come back soon.	bwelbampronto↓	Vuelvan pronto.
15 Goodbye.	adyos↓	Adiós.

4.3 COMPLEX INTONATION PATTERNS

The listing of simple intonation patterns in the previous section is undoubtedly incomplete, although most of the common patterns are included. Complex patterns are, for the most part, combinations and arrangements of simple patterns. The combinations can be considerably complex in the whole sentence and still quite simple in the individual phrases.

An example to illustrate utterances containing several similar patterns is a listing of items in a series. Note the following possibilities:

únò ↑ dós ↑ trés ↑ kwátrò ↑ şíŋkò ↓
óŋşê | dóşê | tréşê | kàtórşê | kíŋşê ↓
sìn.ìŋklwírlúş | ágwà | nìgás ↓

The following drill combines three patterns that are individually different. Together they represent a very common sentence pattern which has two single bar junctures /|/ in the middle of the utterance and a terminal falling juncture /↓/ at the end.

4.31 A COMMON THREE-PHRASE SENTENCE PATTERN

Instructions.—Mimic your model's pronunciation of the utterances in the following column, paying particular attention to the features of intonation.

Pronunciation /1 2 2 2	1 1 2 2	2 2 1 1 ↓/	Spelling
1 loabla|ilopronunşya|muybyen↓	Lo habla y lo pronuncia muy bien.
2 trabahan|enlaembahada|amerikana↓	Trabajan en la embajada americana.
3 elechoes|kenosabemoz|laleksyon↓	El hecho es que no sabemos la lección.
4 dondekeda|labenida|sanmartin↓	¿Dónde queda la avenida San Martín?
5 figurese|kenlamia|somozdyeş↓	Figúrese que la mía somos diez.
6 elmio|seskribe|kombelarga↓	El mío se escribe con be larga.
7 yotrabahe|dos.aṇyos|embogota↓	Yo trabajé dos años en Bogotá.

Pronunciation /1 2 2 2 | 1 1 2 2 | 2 2 1 1 ↓/	Spelling
8 unamuchacha | kebyene | todozloshwebes↓	Una muchacha que viene todos los jueves.
9 kreo | kestasonando | eltelefono↓	Creo que está sonando el teléfono.
10 inorresibyo | elkable | kelemande↓	Y no recibió el cable que le mandé.
11 tubimos | umbyahe̦ | eks(s)elente↓	Tuvimos un viaje excelente.
12 noskedamos | unozdias | ensantyago↓	Nos quedamos unos días en Santiago.
13 yobeŋgo | porustedes | alaznwebe↓	Yo vengo por ustedes a las nueve.
14 anosotros | nospare̦se̦ | muykomoda↓	A nosotros nos parece muy cómoda.
15 nopwedo | ofre̦se̦rle | mazde̦syen↓	No puedo ofrecerle más de cien.

Up to this point in the text, features of pronunciation, whether of vowels or consonants, or of intonation, have been illustrated and drilled in isolated words, phrases, or sentences. Since the most logical function of language is communication, it would seem that such citation forms are somewhat unnatural, that the language in context might provide a more nearly valid sample for discussion.

It is true that out of context a language sample either sounds strange (and therefore not convincingly natural) or adapts to the somewhat stilted patterns of citation forms (and then in reality loses the spontaneity of natural conversation).

We believe that it was necessary and profitable to explain and drill single features of pronunciation, even at the risk of a certain degree of unnaturalness, since many of these features are an obligatory part of speaking Spanish (the /d/ between vowels must be [d], for example). If these obligatory features are sufficiently well drilled so a student can really produce them without thinking about them and making a conscious effort to produce them correctly, he is ready to "think in the language," that is to say, he is ready to apply his conscious efforts to those phases of the language which are optional: what to say, which sentence type to employ, how to use emphasis and contrast, how to "speak between the lines," in other words, to do with Spanish what he is able to do with English.

There are two serious problems involved: (1) how to "internalize" or make completely automatic the obligatory features of the language, in regard both to pronunciation and to grammar, so effectively that they will carry over into real conversation; and (2) how to learn the more subtle features of pronunciation that enhance the efficiency of communication.

Both problems are attacked in the classroom in the same way, by guided practice of authentic language models. But the emphasis can be somewhat different. The first problem, mastering the specific individual features of pronunciation, can be brought into focus through drills built on comparison or contrast patterns, as in this text. Each feature is practiced individually and in context, until correct articulations are second nature. Then there must be a check on the carry-over of these articulations in situations where other features are being emphasized, and corrective measures must be taken when necessary.

The second problem must be met by a situation where the student's attention is focused on all the pronunciation features at once, where interaction and communication are uppermost in the learning process. This implies language in context. The most effective pedagogical tool for this objective is a good dialogue, an intermixture of people and situations. A student who memorizes the lines and parts of a pedagogical dialogue can not only observe the language in action but participate personally, by playing various roles, in realistic communication.

We pointed out in the Introduction that this text is intended to be supplementary, that a complete course should include other materials. At least one part of this complete course should consist of realistic dialogues in which a student can see the operation of the language in a total communication system in which not only the words and language patterns but also cultural values of Hispanic civilization are illustrated and utilized. It is true that part of the justification for studying a foreign language is the opportunity to learn about other people in different cultural backgrounds, and there is no reason why this background information should not be included in the text materials of the language classroom.

The ingredients of good pronunciation have all been supplied in the preceding exercises, but we should like to add one drill where they are combined. The following dialogue can serve as a sample of the kind of performance which is the ultimate aim of language teaching.

4.32 LANGUAGE IN CONTEXT

Instructions.—Mimic your model's pronunciation of the following dialogue sentences. Practice them until you are able to produce the entire sequence without prompting. Be prepared to play any of the three roles.

	Pronunciation	Spelling
John:	oye↓ dan│estasfyestas.aki│	Oye, ¿dan estas fiestas aquí
	muyamenudo↓	muy a menudo?

Pronunciation	Spelling
José: no↓ solo|debes.eŋkwando↓ porke↓	No, sólo de vez en cuando, ¿por qué?
John: esta|meparese̦|estupenda↓	Esta me parece estupenda.
fihate|komo̦estabaylando|	Fíjate como está bailando
esamorena↓	esa morena.
José: kwidado↓ nobayas|ameterlapata↓	¡Cuidado, no vayas a meter la pata!
ezla̦iha|delseŋyordelakasa↓	Es la hija del señor de la casa.
Carmen: mira↓ yokreia|kelos.amerikanos	Mira, yo creía que los americanos
eranmastraŋkilos↓	eran más tranquilos.
José: esekepasa|porai↑	Ese que pasa por ahí
es.elkoronelharris↓	es el Coronel Harris.
ben↑ itelopresento↓	Ven y te lo presento.
John: muybyen↓ selo̦agradesko↓	Muy bien, se lo agradezco.
José: bweno|chikas↓ kompermiso↓	Bueno, chicas. Con permiso.
ensegida|bolbemos↓	En seguida volvemos.

4.4 | SUMMING-UP OF INTONATION

As we have seen, intonation is a complex of the features of stress, pitch, and juncture. Each of these features can be isolated by analysis, described, illustrated, and drilled. Together they carry an important part of the message of any sentence. With variation only in the intonation pattern, the same sentence may enthusiastically affirm or categorically deny what the sum of its words purport:

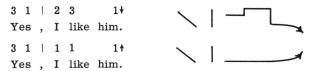

```
3  1  |  2  3      1↓
Yes ,  I  like  him.

3  1  |  1  1      1↑
Yes ,  I  like  him.
```

Intonation features are present in every utterance. No sentence can be pronounced without stress, pitch, and juncture, and if they are partially removed or distorted, communication can be very difficult. There are other features of pronunciation which also affect the meaning of a sentence, for example, overloudness, oversoftness, overfast or overslow tempo, drawling, clipping, rasp, openness. These features, sometimes referred to as vocalizations, are not structured in the same way as intonation features are. It is important to identify vocalizations mainly so that they may be separated from intonation; otherwise it is almost impossible to understand either. Intonation features are structured and separable; both in English and in Spanish there is a definite number of levels of pitch and degrees of stress, but there is an unbroken continuum of overloudness, oversoftness, etc.

Fortunately the vocalizations are sufficiently similar in Spanish and English (both in form and meaning) that they do not cause any serious trouble for a student crossing this linguistic boundary in either direction. If the vowels, the consonants, and the intonations are mastered, the vocalizations may reasonably be expected to fall neatly into place.

PHONETIC SYMBOLS

CONSONANTS

[b]	baile, vamos
[ƀ]	iba, uva
[ch]	Chile
[d]	donde
[đ]	adonde, cada
[f]	fósforo
[g]	guerra, gato
[g̶]	lago
[h]	jota, gira
[ʰ]	este
[k]	kilo, casa, que
[l]	lima
[(l)ɏ]	llama
[m]	mano
[n]	no
[n.V]	[ŋV] in some dialects, [nV] in others: en esto
[ŋ]	cinco
[ny]	año
[p]	pase
[r]	pero
[rr]	rosa, perro
[s]	sabe
[s.V]	[ʰV] in some dialects, [sV] in others: es Ana
[ş]	zapatos, cerveza
[t]	taza
[w]	puerta, causa
[y]	fierro, rey
[ɏ]	ya, vaya
[z]	mismo, desde
[ẓ]	juzgar

VOWELS

[a]	pa̱so
[e]	pe̱so
[ɛ]	pe̱ste
[i]	pi̱so
[o]	po̱so
[u]	pu̱so
[V̆]	very short vowel, as in "de̱ Ana" (3 syllables)
[V̠]	non-syllabic, as in "de̱ Ana" (2 syllables)

INTONATION

[↑]	rising termination: ¿Ya se va? (⟋)
[↓]	falling termination: Sí, ya me voy. (⟍)
[ǀ]	level termination: Sí (→) ya me voy.
[v́]	strong stress
[v̆]	weak stress
[3]	high pitch
[2]	middle pitch
[1]	low pitch

ADDITIONAL SYMBOLS FOR ENGLISH

[j]	ju̱dge
[š]	she̱
[ž]	mea̱sure
[ɨ]	ju̱st (adv.), rose̱s
[æ]	bla̱nk
[ɪ]	bi̱t
[ɔ]	co̱st
[v̀]	(medial stress) cóntràctòr

INDEX